T0029664

Masters at Work

BECOMING A
SOCIAL WORKER

MASTERS AT WORK

BECOMING A SOCIAL WORKER

ALEX ABRAMOVICH

AND TASHA BLAINE

SIMON & SCHUSTER

New York   London   Toronto   Sydney   New Delhi

Simon & Schuster
1230 Avenue of the Americas
New York, NY 10020

First Simon & Schuster hardcover edition March 2021

SIMON & SCHUSTER and colophon are registered trademarks of
Simon & Schuster, Inc.

For information about special discounts for bulk purchases,
please contact Simon & Schuster Special Sales at 1-866-506-1949
or business@simonandschuster.com

The Simon & Schuster Speakers Bureau can bring authors to your
live event. For more information or to book an event contact the
Simon & Schuster Speakers Bureau at 1-866-248-3049
or visit our website at www.simonspeakers.com.

Manufactured in the United States of America

1   3   5   7   9   10   8   6   4   2

Library of Congress Cataloging-in-Publication Data is available

ISBN 978-1-9821-4037-3
ISBN 978-1-9821-4040-3 (ebook)

FOR SUSAN MAYE

CONTENTS

BECOMING A
SOCIAL WORKER

INTRODUCTION

Social workers are frontline workers, counseling families in crisis, helping survivors of domestic violence, finding foster homes for children. They may be overburdened, overtired, overextended, and overwhelmed—but rarely do social workers get bored.

It's hard to be bored when you're working with people at their most open, unguarded, and vulnerable. Social workers do a great many things: they are substance abuse counselors at celebrity rehab centers and psychotherapists in private practice; they staff abortion clinics and homeless shelters; they're caseworkers just out of college and high-level administrators with decades' worth of experience under their belts. Social workers work in courtrooms and hospitals; at Ivy League universities and inner-city high schools; on military bases; in nursing and residential care facilities; in corporate human resources departments and labor union offices.

Social workers help shape public policy at city, state, and federal levels. In the field, they conduct research (one-on-one interviews, focus groups, surveys) that influences our understanding of social formations and the human mind. In fact, those two poles—social formations and the human mind—are the things social workers find themselves balancing daily, because social work is rooted in the idea that individuals are inseparable from their environments.

Social work is an ever-expanding profession: if there's a void—some systemic social problem that isn't being addressed—social workers rush in to fill the vacuum. As a result, the U.S. Bureau of Labor Statistics estimates, the profession is expected to grow by 13 percent by the end of the 2020s—much faster than the average for all other occupations.

But what *are* social workers, exactly? What kind of work do they do?

According to the National Association of Social Workers, "the primary mission of the social work profession is to enhance human well-being and help meet the basic human needs of all people, with particular attention to the needs and empowerment of people who are vulnerable, oppressed, and living in poverty."

What this means is that social workers advocate for individuals and ensure that their most fundamental needs—nutrition, education, health, and mental health care—are being met. At the same time, social workers fight for social justice and change.

In day-to-day terms social workers work collaboratively with clients to determine their goals, help them navigate bureaucratic systems, and offer emotional support. They provide referrals and connect clients to basic resources, such as housing, health care, education, mental health care, and/or public assistance. Whether or not they work as therapists, social workers may also find themselves providing psychotherapeutic services. And in crisis situations, such as domestic violence and child abuse, social workers step in to deescalate the problem and provide safety.

A client who's had all their needs met, or now has the ability to meet their own needs, no longer requires a social worker. A society that is perfectly fair, just, and equitable would have no use for social workers, either. In that sense, the social worker's ultimate goal is to render their own job obsolete.

THERE'S NO ONE PATH to becoming a social worker. At the undergraduate level, aspiring social workers can earn a bachelor of social work (BSW) degree. But it's not unusual for social workers to major in English, psychology, sociology, or other subjects. Nor is it unusual for social workers to come to the job after working in another profession. In social work, lived experience counts, and a BSW is not a requirement for graduate school.

In graduate school, students generally complete foundational courses in human behavior and the social environment, research, and social welfare policy before choosing a track or concentration. Most programs offer concentrations in clinical practice (mental health), generalist practice (administration, community organizing, and program development), and policy practice (research, policy analysis, and policy advocacy). Along with their coursework, students are expected to complete two internships ("field placements"), working three days a week in schools, hospitals, nonprofits, city agencies, or community health centers, carrying caseloads, receiving supervision, and gaining intensive hands-on training. Interns are also required to complete weekly process recordings, writing sessions out verbatim while describing their thoughts in the margins. While these documents are time-consuming and tedious to write, they are also tremendously useful. In the course of reviewing them, supervisors offer feedback on the students' responses to clients, critiquing questions and noting instances of bias and projection.

Typically, social workers complete their programs in two years, graduating with a master of social work (MSW) degree. Afterward many will complete state exams to become a licensed master social worker (LMSW)—a necessary step for employment at some agencies. In order to become clinical social workers, who provide therapy and counseling to individuals and/or groups, they must complete approximately 2,000 hours of direct therapeutic work with clients under the supervision of a licensed clinical social worker. They then take a clinical licensing exam and become a licensed clinical social worker

(LCSW), which allows them to open a private therapy practice.

After graduation and licensing, social workers grow into a wide variety of jobs, from therapist to researcher to director of clinical services, in any number of settings, such as schools, hospitals, prisons, mental health clinics, medical clinics, private practice, nonprofits, government agencies, and child welfare agencies. The populations a social worker encounters might include families and children (often those living in poverty), people with disabilities, and people suffering from substance abuse problems or mental illness. Social workers serve the elderly, immigrants, and refugees, but they also work with middle-class and even prosperous clients. The field is remarkably broad—it offers a wealth of employment opportunities—and yet, there are several things social workers have in common.

Social workers are passionate about people, passionate about social justice, and passionate about the work that they do. They are strong advocates for individuals who may not be able to advocate for themselves. Social workers are natural problem-solvers, and empathetic ones, able to see each issue from several perspectives. They are active listeners as well as critical thinkers. All social workers are trained to follow these guiding principles:

- person-in-environment approach
- meeting the client where they are
- strengths-based perspective (resilience)
- cultural consciousness
- social and economic justice

Here's what those principles mean in practice:

Person-in-environment approach. The idea of assessing individuals within the context of their specific social environments is central to social work. Social workers believe that people are inseparable from the environments in which they were raised, and in which they live and work now.

Meeting the client where they are. Social workers don't push their clients to change; they know that doing so can be counterproductive and often backfires. Instead, social workers adapt to move at the client's own pace and encourage them to come up with their own plan of treatment.

Strengths-based perspective (resilience). Social workers focus on their clients' determination and resiliency, their aspirations, and their assets. On an interpersonal level this may involve an assessment of clients' support networks, their families, and/or their faith. On a societal level it may involve a judgment-free approach to stigmatized populations, such as the homeless and those who struggle with substance abuse.

Cultural consciousness. Social workers are expected to examine their own backgrounds and biases, their values, and personal assumptions. They strive to be aware of their privileges and powers so that they can approach clients with cultural humility and—as they work with specific populations—study the norms and values of those populations without consciously or unconsciously imposing their own beliefs.

Social and economic justice. Social workers empower individuals and groups to strive for economic equity and social equality. They are committed to community outreach, grassroots organizing, and lobbying.

All of these principles are foundational to social work going all the way back to the profession's beginnings.

SOCIAL WORK AS IT is practiced in the United States has its roots in nineteenth-century Europe. Elizabeth Fry visited Newgate Prison in London in 1813 and, appalled by what she saw there, worked tirelessly (and successfully) to effect prison reform in England. At around the same time, a Scottish clergyman named Thomas Chalmers started working with the urban poor in Glasgow, making home visits, strengthening community ties, and ensuring that children received secular as well as religious educations. Jean Henry Dunant, a Swiss businessman, established the Red Cross in 1863 and organized the Geneva Convention in 1864; he was awarded the first Nobel Peace Prize in 1901.

Eighteen sixty-four was also the year that another English reformer, Octavia Hill, started buying dilapidated houses in London to facilitate the care and empowerment of her poor, often unemployed tenants. Hill believed that it made no sense to work with an impoverished population without taking environmental concerns like housing and education into account. She encouraged her assistants to form personal relationships with tenants in order to work toward bettering their lives.

Arnold Toynbee, who taught economic history at Oxford (and was an uncle of the historian Arnold J. Toynbee), was also decades ahead of his time. Toynbee—who popularized the phrase "industrial revolution"—believed that industrialization had produced "wealth without producing well-being." He opened libraries for industrial workers, encouraged students to work directly with underserved populations, and worked himself to death before reaching his thirty-first birthday. A year later, in 1884, the first settlement house opened in the East End of London. Named Toynbee Hall in his honor, it housed poor students from Oxford and Cambridge and provided a number of social services, including courses in nursing, writing, sewing, citizenship, and hygiene.

Three years later, in Chicago, a woman named Jane Addams read an article about Toynbee Hall. In 1888, she and her partner, Ellen Gates Starr, traveled to London to see it for themselves. Deeply impressed, Addams and Starr established Hull House in Chicago. This was the first American settlement house.

At Hull House immigrants from Bohemia, Ireland, Italy, Germany, Greece, Poland, and Russia could take English classes and American government, cooking, and music. Working mothers had access to an in-house kindergarten and day care center. Hull House hosted an employment bureau, an art gallery, a girls' club, a fitness center, a library, and a theater. It provided job training for unskilled workers and temporary foster care for children. Settlement houses started to spring up in cities all over the country. By 1910 there were more than four hundred. By 1920 there were close to five hundred.

Settlement houses were instrumental in ending child labor and establishing juvenile courts. The United States Children's Bureau was started by the leaders of Hull House in 1912 and run by a Hull House alumna named Julia Lathrop; in 1913 it launched its first research program, investigating infant mortality. The settlement houses viewed populations they served in terms of their environments, endeavoring to provide them with the means to lift themselves out of poverty.

Social work as a profession came into its own at the turn of the century, when universities started to offer social work courses. Columbia University in New York City offered the first in 1898; six years later, in 1904, Harvard University and Simmons College started the Boston School for Social Workers; and in 1905, Massachusetts General Hospital in Boston hired the first professional medical social workers. Before long, professional social workers were being employed by hospitals in cities all over the country, in public schools, and in juvenile courts.

Until the Great Depression, however, social work was still the province of community-based, municipal, and statewide service providers. It took the New Deal to establish the federal government as a source of aid and education, and it did so on a grand scale. By the end of the 1930s the number of social workers in America had doubled, from 40,000 to 80,000, and after the Second World War the profession's ranks swelled again, with social workers addressing the needs of returning veterans (as they had done previously, at the end of the First World War, when the Red Cross had asked social workers to treat veterans suffering from what was known then as "shell shock"). More and more, social workers found themselves working with clients on issues relating to mental health, taking on roles traditionally associated with psychotherapists—when interest in therapy and personal growth ballooned in the 1960s, social workers were well-placed and well qualified to shift gears and go into private practice as therapists.

FOR ALL THE GOOD that social workers do, many stereotypes remain entrenched: Social workers are poorly paid. Social workers think emotionally, not critically or realistically. Social workers are powerless to effect meaningful change.

In this book you will meet three social workers who buck every one of these stereotypes.

Laura Fernandez began her career thirty years ago as a caseworker in Boston. Back then she did not have a master's degree. Today she runs a clinical staff of ninety at Sanctuary for Families, New York's leading provider of services and advocacy for survivors of domestic violence. Laura's path from caseworker to supervisor to program head is a classic career trajectory for a successful social worker. Her belief that real, quantifiable change can take place at the individual, organizational, and societal levels is rooted in her biography, in her experiences, and in the achievements of people she's helped.

John Barr investigates overdose deaths for the New York City Office of the Chief Medical Examiner. He came to social work later in life; for John, it's a second career. But John is also an example of the way social workers get better with age. His own vast store of experiences, combined with his thoughtful approach to the job, helps to answer some of the profession's most challenging questions: What happens when a social worker's values don't align with the core purpose of the organization they're working within? What are the job's limits when a social worker comes up against institutional intransigence?

Wendy Doucette is a psychotherapist in Los Angeles who has spent years building a private practice from scratch, working one-on-one with individual clients. Her section gives us the opportunity to see a social worker inside the therapy room, guiding clients as they find their own paths out of depression, disquiet, and childhood trauma, and move toward peace and stability. Here, and throughout, we have combined attributes of real-life clients to create composite characters. (Sharwline Nicholson, who appears in Laura's section, is an exception because her story has become part of the public record.) But in each instance the issues and problems we see these clients encounter are specific, true-to-life, and faithful to our subjects' backgrounds and ways of working.

As you'll see, the work can be tough, demanding, and heartbreaking—and yet it is deeply fulfilling. Social workers do heroic things. They listen to people in pain and fight for resources and change. They are part of the glue that holds society together and part of the dream and the promise of better societies to come.

1

LAURA FERNANDEZ

Laura Fernandez works in a carefully restored Beaux-Arts building with televisions in the elevators and a swanky rooftop lounge. The grand lobby has high vaulted ceilings, marble floors, and gold-leaf rosettes on the walls. The company directory lists blue-chip law firms and boutique marketing companies. But there is no entry for Laura's employer, Sanctuary for Families.

Sanctuary serves one of New York City's most vulnerable populations: victims of domestic violence. Its official address is a post office box; only the agency's staff and clients know the physical location. We don't know ourselves until the morning we're due to meet Laura, who is Sanctuary's clinical director. After taking an elevator up to a nondescript office, we are instructed by a receptionist sitting behind a glass partition to take a seat in the otherwise empty waiting room.

Five minutes later Laura appears. She is a compact middle-aged woman with shoulder-length hair, big brown eyes, a warm smile. Back in the eighties, she tells us, Sanctuary for Families was run out of a church parish house in midtown Manhattan. The agency had only five employees. Since then Sanctuary has grown to become New York State's largest nonprofit provider of services for victims of domestic violence and sex trafficking as well as for child victims and witnesses. Sanctuary runs women's shelters in each of the city's five boroughs. (One of those shelters, the Sarah Burke House, is the largest transitional center for domestic violence survivors in New York State.) The agency operates out of five family justice centers as well, and runs a multiservice walk-in center for sex workers and survivors of sexual violence (including victims of genital mutilation). It provides what is known as wraparound care—crisis intervention, emergency and transitional shelter, career services, legal assistance and representation, counseling, and long-term follow-up services—for ten thousand adults and children each year. Put more simply, the agency helps victims get away from their abusers and assists them as they rebuild their lives as survivors. The challenges that Laura and her colleagues face day in and day out are staggering. Eighty-two percent of Sanctuary's clients live in poverty. Three-quarters of them are immigrants. Many of them speak no English at all.

As we walk through a maze of cubicles, Laura talks about the agency's shift to an open floor plan. "The staff definitely didn't like that transition," she says with a shrug and a smile. What the shrug seems to be saying is *Change is hard all around, but I'm willing to accept the blowback if it means the changes are good.*

"It's hard to work that way, I understand," Laura continues. "Before, everyone had their own little office. But now that they're all in the open, the people working here interact more. They come to each other with their concerns. They talk problems through together."

Laura herself is chatty, direct. She took the Myers-Briggs personality test once, but it only told her what she already knew: she's an off-the-charts extrovert. Talking things out is how she herself tends to solve problems, and the problems and challenges Laura has faced in her three decades on the job have been significant.

Over thirty years ago, in Boston, Laura took her first social work job as a child welfare caseworker. Twenty-eight years ago she started at Columbia University's School of Social Work; Sanctuary for Families was her second-year internship. Upon graduation, Sanctuary hired her as a full-time women's counselor. After three years of doing that work she left Sanctuary and took a position at Edwin Gould Services for Children and Families, an agency contracted by the New York City Administration for Children's Services to provide child welfare services, including foster care. She spent the next sixteen years at Edwin Gould, working up to assistant executive director of programs before Sanctuary lured her back in 2015 to be their clinical director.

In a way, returning to Sanctuary felt like a homecoming. The clinical director Laura replaced had been with the agency for more than two decades; Laura had worked under her as an intern and a counselor. Now Laura was responsible for a team of ninety; for all of Sanctuary's clinical services, including counseling, case management, and crisis intervention; and for the department's $5.8 million budget. She also oversees the quality of treatment for thousands of clients, all of whom are victims of chronic trauma, which Laura had seen plenty of as a caseworker.

"In my early child welfare years," she says, "back when

I was seeing horrors firsthand, my friends graduated from college and told happy stories and I would tell stories about death, molestation, violence. They would be, like, 'You're so dark.' And it was. It completely consumed me, those first few years of doing the work. Then I thought: *I cannot be doing this. When I'm not at work, I can't be driving down the street, thinking a client is going to die and I didn't do anything, thinking that I didn't save them.* I found ways to compartmentalize years ago—ways to put that piece away. I realized I *can't* save them. It's their journey. They have to save themselves. Over time I have also seen clients who have gone through really bad stuff come out the other side and be okay. I've learned that can happen. Even people who go through the darkest things can come out the other side."

Laura still recalls those dark, riveting stories from her days in the trenches as a child welfare worker. They may be compartmentalized but, given the opportunity, old clients come rushing back: the four-year-old boy whose stepfather had beaten him so severely that his retina had become detached, leaving him legally blind; the eleven-year-old girl who had lived with the same foster family for ten years and then been kicked to the curb suddenly with no explanation.

Working in child welfare gave Laura her first sense of the ways in which institutions designed to help people—schools, social service agencies, and the courts—can actually hurt and dehumanize them. And while her days of working directly with clients are behind her, Laura now works tirelessly to transform the systems that serve them. Her daily duties—answering emails, taking calls, attending strategy meetings, drafting and reviewing documents—may seem mundane but they have the potential to shape the experience of every one of the thousands of clients Sanctuary works with each year.

SOCIAL WORK IS DIVIDED into three tiers of practice: micro, mezzo, and macro.

Micro social work practice is what most people picture social work to be: counseling single mothers, aiding children, visiting the elderly. The job is direct and one-on-one. At the micro level a social worker might work in a shelter with homeless clients. But a clinical social worker in private practice who treats upper-middle-class clients falls into the same category. It doesn't matter who the client is, only that the social worker is interacting with an individual.

Mezzo social work practice broadens the scope, looking to effect change for small groups or communities. A mezzo social worker might facilitate therapeutic groups, run trainings, or develop health-care initiatives in tandem with a local clinic.

Macro social workers deal with constructs and large populations. They develop programs that target specific groups, advocate on the legislative level, and push for concrete policy shifts.

What the three tiers have in common is the end goal: all social workers strive to improve functioning for their clients while ensuring that their basic needs—housing, education, health care, and personal safety—are being met. Some social workers jump between levels as a matter of course in the span of one day. Others start at the micro level and work their way up. Laura, for instance, was already thinking in macro terms when she was still a caseworker and counselor, thanks in part to her interest in politics, poverty, and systems, but also in response to personal encounters with individual clients—women like Sharwline Nicholson, who made a lasting impression.

"I was working as a women's counselor at Sanctuary when Sharwline came in," Laura recalls. "She'd been referred to Sanctuary by an outside law firm."

Nicholson was thirty-two years old when she and Laura first met. She worked full-time as a cashier at Home Depot while pursuing a full-time degree in behavioral science, and she had a boyfriend, Claude Barnett, who drove up from South Carolina once a month to visit her and Destinee, the baby girl they'd had together. During one of those visits, Nicholson broke up with Barnett, telling him that the long-distance relationship no longer worked. Barnett had never assaulted Nicholson, but now he flew into a rage, cracking Nicholson's skull, fracturing her ribs, and breaking one of her arms before fleeing. Bruised and bloodied, she called 911 and asked a neighbor to come take care of Destinee, who was in her crib at the time, and Nicholson's son, Kendell, who was at school. The neighbor, who had babysat for the children before, agreed to watch Destinee and pick Kendell up at his school bus stop.

That night in the hospital, Nicholson gave police officers the names of relatives who could come get her children and take care of them. But the next day she was informed that the Administration for Children's Services (ACS) had taken custody of Destinee and Kendell. The children were in "imminent risk if they remained in the care of Ms. Nicholson because she was not at the time able to protect herself nor her children because Mr. Barnett had viciously beaten her," ACS had determined.

Nicholson hired a lawyer. She appeared several times in family court. Eight days after she had last seen her children—who had since been placed in foster care—she was finally allowed a visit with them. At the ACS foster care agency in Queens, Nicholson followed the sound of Destinee's crying and located her in a room by herself. The baby had a rash on her face, her nose was running, and she appeared to have scratched herself.

Kendell had a swollen eye: his foster mother had slapped him, he told Nicholson.

Nicholson demanded a phone with which to call the police. ACS denied the request but did agree to a new foster mother. When that woman arrived, Kendell asked, "You are not going to hit me, are you?"

Four days later Kendell turned six. Nicholson was not allowed to see or speak with him on his birthday.

"It took Sharwline twenty-one days to get her children back," Laura recalls. "But the court was demanding that she move out of her home and into a shelter. Sharwline didn't want to."

Nicholson's boyfriend had left the state once again. She felt that she wasn't in danger and she didn't want to bring her children to a shelter. "Back then," Laura explains, "survivors of domestic violence had to do certain things, whether it was logical or not logical for their individual situations. But Nicholson's whole situation was extremely messed up."

One of Sharwline's children received disability payments, and those funds had gone straight to the foster care agency; that had happened immediately, but getting the funds back was taking an eternity. She'd lost her job. She'd been in school, and she had to drop out.

Laura says, "Sharwline kept asking, 'How could this have happened to me? I was a victim. I did nothing wrong. I called the police. I sent my kids to the neighbor's. I called my family.' What she cared about, most of all, was making her experience mean something. 'I want to change the system,' she'd say. Even though her whole life had been blown apart, her biggest focus was on preventing the same thing from happening to other people. She focused on systemic changes immediately. For starters, she wanted child welfare workers to get better training. And eventually it led to a whole class action suit. It took a long time to work its way through the courts, but I became an expert witness in that case.

"I had seen victims of domestic violence who had put their children at risk," Laura says. "I had seen cases where there were reasons for child welfare to get involved. But what I was *really* seeing back then was that people who'd done everything by the book ended up losing their kids anyway. I saw case planners tell women to 'give the guy another chance'—that was something they'd actually put in their notes. Or child welfare services would get involved and the woman would end up with a service plan a mile long while the father got sent to anger management. I would think, 'He's the one that needs all those services! He needs parenting. He needs therapy. But you're putting it all on the mother!' Everything, then, was about blaming mothers, and those were all things that I got to talk about on the stand. From my vantage point, as someone who had been a child welfare worker and worked in domestic violence, I described ways that the child welfare system wasn't helping the people that it was supposed to protect. I told the court, even within the limits of the child welfare system we could have been doing much better."

Almost five years after the incident, in 2004, the United States District Court, Eastern District of New York, ruled that a woman's inability to protect her children from witnessing abuse did not constitute neglect and could not be the basis for that child's removal. In a long, scathing decision, Judge Jack B. Weinstein found that ACS had violated Nicholson's rights under the Fourth, Ninth, Thirteen, Fourteenth, and Nineteenth Amendments to the Bill of Rights and compared Nicholson's treatment by ACS to the way Black women had been treated under slavery.

"The evidence reveals widespread and unnecessary cruelty by agencies of the City of New York towards mothers abused by their consorts . . . ," Weinstein decided. "The pitiless double abuse of these mothers is not malicious, but is due to benign indifference, bureaucratic inefficiency, and outmoded institutional biases."

Survivors of domestic violence would no longer be treated as criminals, and ACS was charged with helping them to find shelter and file orders of protection against their abusers. The New York State Court of Appeals went further and ruled that, prior to removing any child from their home, ACS and the family courts had to weigh the psychological harm caused by such a removal against the potential harm of letting the child remain in place.

These were landmark cases—rulings that transformed the way ACS operates in New York State as a whole—and Laura's testimony helped ensure the verdicts.

SOCIAL WORKERS ARE DRAWN to the field for all kinds of reasons. Some have their own histories of trauma and bring a heightened sense of empathy and understanding to their work with clients. Others are motivated by a strong sense of justice and human rights and an abiding concern for under-represented and vulnerable populations. Some social workers are pulled to the variety of work settings and people they might encounter, along with the job security that an ever-expanding profession like social work provides. Still others were directly impacted by a social worker in their own lives and recognize the inherent meaning and necessity of the profession. But at first Laura Fernandez had no intention of becoming a social worker at all.

Laura had moved to Boston after graduating from Tufts and taking a job in Governor Michael Dukakis's office. But Dukakis was a lame duck with six months left on the job, and when those six months were up, Laura's job ended too. In the meanwhile, a close friend of Laura's had gone to work for the Massachusetts Department of Social Services. Laura told herself, *There's no way I could do that.* The friend had a degree in sociology; Laura had double-majored in history and French. But the prospect of having to go on unemployment led Laura to reconsider and apply for a position as a caseworker.

"What would you do if you went into a home and there was a gun on the table?" the interviewer asked her.

Laura's first thought was *I would get the hell out of there!* Then she decided, *No, that can't be the right answer.*

"I would assess everyone's safety," she said instead.

"No," the interviewer told her. "You would get out of there!"

Then, just like that, the woman gave Laura a job.

In a field like child welfare, where the burnout rate is high, there is incredible demand for caseworkers. This was especially true in 1990, when the crack epidemic and the AIDS crisis were raging and foster care systems all over the country were flooded and falling apart. Some children stayed in care for eighteen years, in placements that were never deemed permanent. Others got completely lost in the system, shuttling from bad situations to worse. On her first day Laura pictured herself as Lindsay Wagner in *The Bionic Woman*. The bionic woman had long, blown-out hair. She wore sharp outfits. But she was a therapist, too. By the end of her first day Laura had discovered no one looked like that in child welfare. It was hot and sweaty in the projects; you had to wear comfortable clothes. The city also required that, for hygienic reasons, caseworkers like Laura wear gloves.

"Everyone thought they were going to get AIDS," she recalls. "There was a real sense of danger. We were especially careful around children in diapers. We worried about saliva. We washed everything."

Casework is foundational to social work. It can be grueling, both physically and emotionally. Typically a caseworker spends one to three years in the field before becoming a supervisor, but the things she might learn in those years last a lifetime, and a good social worker can learn more in the course of a single home visit than she would in an entire semester of coursework. The job is a crash course in human behavior.

Laura was expected to conduct safety inspections of foster homes, interview foster parents, and monitor foster kids. She did the same with birth parents. She kept track of every child's medical, dental, and mental health visits, managed school-related issues, and attended special education meetings. Were the birth parents working on their service plan, and making progress? Were they taking their medication? Had they secured appropriate housing and completed their anger management classes, parenting classes, and drug treatment programs? Laura put the answers in her court reports, attended hearings, and testified as a witness when the need arose. And in addition to her daily tasks, there were constant emergencies: children getting kicked out of their foster homes; teens in violent romantic relationships; teens who got pregnant; school suspensions and expulsions; medical emergencies; mental health emergencies; violent outbursts.

There was a girl on Laura's caseload who'd been born out of incest and sexually abused in her home. In foster care, she became volatile and was expelled from one home after another. She needed high-quality treatment immediately or no foster family would agree to keep her.

"I knew about this amazing partial hospitalization program," Laura says. "You had to be in the hospital during the week and home on the weekend. The foster parent the girl had just then didn't drive, but I really wanted her in that program. For three months, every weekend, I drove her myself. I wanted her to have that opportunity. She was blowing through homes, and I knew she needed to be stable." In the end that girl was adopted. But in child welfare happy endings were rare.

Laura remembers four siblings from Haiti. Their parents had died of AIDS and the children were split up and sent into different homes. Once a month, Laura picked them up one at a time and drove them to see each other. She took them to the movies and to McDonald's.

She took them to eat Haitian food, too, and ate goat herself for the very first time.

She did what she could to keep the siblings connected.

Laura learned all the old social work tricks: In the projects, take the elevator, not the stairs. Tell families that you're allergic to pit bulls so that they'll keep theirs in the other room. If there's hoarding, don't sit down—unless you want to bring home bedbugs. Wear headphones in rough neighborhoods so you can pretend you're not hearing the catcalls, but leave the music off and remain fully aware of your environment.

Most importantly, don't make promises of any kind that you won't be able to keep. The children you're working with have had enough disappointments already.

"There I was, twenty-two, and I was deciding whether people should keep their kids," Laura reflects. "I mean, they sent us to some useless training, but it doesn't prepare you for what you see once you're in the home."

One of the very first cases she worked on involved a mother with borderline personality disorder. The woman's children bounced off the walls as Laura stood in the living room, trying to get through the visit, and while she was in the middle of asking a question, the woman's four-year-old son lunged at her with a carrot, sticking it so hard in Laura's eye that she thought she'd been blinded.

She left that visit thinking, *I am being attacked by a four-year-old. I'm in way over my head.*

On top of that, Laura had to document every single thing she did in writing. In casework and social work, if you don't document an action, it's as if it never happened. If you call a teacher and don't get an answer, document it. Write: "I left a seventh voice mail." When you have a conversation with a foster parent, document everything that parent said. If you go to the same home ten times in a row and find no one home every time, document it *ten times*. Make sure that your notes on each case are consistent and that every concern you've flagged is addressed. Keep the language neutral and free of all judgment. Don't fall behind or you'll never catch up.

Laura worked in what she calls "the weirdest catchment area you could have had in Boston," covering neighborhoods that were all over the place demographically. Her office was located in a housing project in Charlestown, a poor white area with very high levels of domestic violence.

"There was immense racism in Charlestown, too," she notes. "As I worked with birth families and foster families, I realized that however far they had gone in school synced up with the year desegregation had come to Boston. That was the year they'd dropped out. There was a cross burning in Charlestown when I was there. Black social workers were not even sent into Charlestown."

Laura also covered the North End, Beacon Hill, Chelsea, and Revere. Chelsea was largely Latino immigrants. Revere was home to a population of Vietnamese refugees. There was crushing poverty in these areas, but in Beacon Hill wealthy clients hired lawyers and got away with violence, neglect—everything short of murder. "No one wanted to go to Beacon Hill," Laura remarks. "You weren't going to get anywhere. The injustice, in terms of results and resources, could not have been much more glaring."

Most communities Laura served were completely disconnected from the world she had grown up in—a world where you went to school, got a job, got married, bought a house, raised a family, and retired.

"Do you have kids?" a child in Revere asked her.

"No. I'm not married yet."

"What does marriage have to do with having a kid?"

In Charlestown, Laura told a thirteen-year-old boy, "You need to say no to drugs."

"You don't get to tell me that and go home to your neighborhood," the boy said. "I have to live here. You don't. You can't tell me what to do or how to deal with people out on my street corner."

Laura was embarrassed and humbled by that conversation. She went home and thought, *That boy is right. I* don't *know what it's like, living in his neighborhood. I need to listen to him and help* him *figure out how to be safe in his neighborhood—on his terms.*

Simple and potent, the lessons kept coming. Laura had assumed that if someone dropped out of tenth grade, they'd walked away with the knowledge and skills a high schooler would have. In Boston she learned that grade levels were meaningless: a kid in tenth grade could be reading at the first-grade level. Who was Laura to judge someone in that situation? If she had fallen that far behind, would there have been a reason for *her* to stay in high school?

Laura stopped giving advice and started listening more closely to her clients. She wouldn't have phrased it this way at the time, but she was coming to terms with some basic tenets of social work: seeing the client as inseparable from the specific circumstances of their environment and recognizing their strengths and resilience.

"I still remember that boy in Charlestown," she says. "I still hear him. That voice is always there: Who the hell was *I* to tell him not to do drugs? When he said that, what I really thought was *Who am I?* Who was I in the widest possible sense? My clients were up against massive structural barriers. They went to terrible schools. They had terrible housing. But they got up every day and they lived. I came to admire their resilience. They were very strong, and I needed to figure out how to break down more barriers for them. That's what I took from those early years. My white savior, do-gooder thinking transitioned to 'Wow, all the systems are broken, they are oppressive, and together with my clients I need to fight them and change them.'"

Caseworkers are foot soldiers in the war against systemic inequality and injustice. But by the same token it's all but impossible for caseworkers to implement systemic changes. Laura had kids removed from homes. She helped families stay together. She learned that foster care wasn't an answer; it was a last resort, and after that first year in foster care she transitioned to adoption work. Instead of taking kids out of their homes, she helped them find forever places. That work was easier. There were more inspirational moments. But in order to do more at the macro level Laura knew she would have to go to graduate school. In 1994, after four years of casework in Boston, she enrolled in the master's program at Columbia's School of Social Work and started on her path to becoming a supervisor.

———

WHEN LAURA RETURNED TO Sanctuary, in 2015, the agency's in-house lawyers were valued in ways that its social workers were not. It wasn't hard to see why: the lawyers wore suits. They acted like lawyers. "They were flashier and splashier," Laura admits. The lawyers won high-profile cases, like the landmark case involving Sharwline Nicholson and her children. But, Laura points out, she was deeply involved with Nicholson, too.

"Social workers have a weird inferiority complex," Laura says. "I think it goes back to the fact that we work with poor people. A lot of our work is behind the scenes. It's messy and it's unsung."

This is a recurring theme among social workers: the way the professsion is stigmatized, tarred with the same brush that's used on immigrants and other economically disadvantaged populations. "I am so proud of my social work degree," a social worker might tell you. But in her day-to-day life the same social worker will describe herself as a therapist or psychotherapist—never as a social worker.

Laura was determined to raise the profile of her department's social workers. She believed they deserved the same level of respect—and, crucially, funding—that the agency's lawyers were accustomed to. Sanctuary's clinical services were as solid as they'd ever been, but Laura set new goals for them. For that point on, they would have to be innovative.

In order to do that, she became a powerful advocate before the agency's board of directors, doing her best to shift every member's attention toward childhood development. As she crafted her presentations on early trauma and the powerful impact of positive intervention, she took care to highlight specific cases and outcomes rather than theories, abstractions, and social work platitudes.

It wasn't what the board—a thirty-two-member body comprising mostly lawyers, bankers, and business executives—was used to. But it was extremely effective. Afterward, several board members told Laura they simply hadn't thought in those terms before. "You have to put things in terms that resonate," she reasons. "People don't want all the fluffy, soft stuff. They want compelling narratives. To be an effective leader you have to read the room. You have to speak to your audience."

Laura's efforts to elevate the department were inseparable from the work that she did to transform it. When she had interned at Sanctuary in graduate school, the agency did not have a termination period for its clinical cases. Nor did it have ways to measure improvement: whether clients were reaching their goals; whether treatments were having their desired effect. This had made no sense to Laura back then. Upon her return to Sanctuary, she found that clients were being discharged within three to six months. This made even less sense, given that the agency was still operating without systems that monitored progress. If anything, it was more arbitrary.

Three to six months? Laura thought. *Why* that *amount of time? What's the clinical reason for three to six months?*

The answer, it turned out, was no reason at all.

"For some of our clients," Laura explains, "short-term makes sense. They come in, learn about their rights, learn about domestic violence, and that's all they want. But if a client needs child/parent psychotherapy—if they are having attachment issues—that takes a year and a half to resolve. We see amazing progress, but it takes a long time. If a client has trauma that's complex, or super-complex, three to six months of counseling is not going to be adequate. Cases staying open forever was not a good answer. But measures of progress should have been telling us when to close cases, not the fact that some random amount of time had now passed."

Laura also took stock of her department's children's program, which ran parallel to the adult program but on its own separate track. As a caseworker in Boston and a child welfare supervisor at Edwin Gould, Laura had always seen the family as a unit. But at Sanctuary, upon intake, the adult team assessed the needs of adults and the child team assessed children's needs, with limited collaboration between the two tracks.

If a mother brought her son in for counseling because he was being disruptive in the classroom, had violent outbursts at home, and struggled to relate to his peers—but the mother's own PTSD was off the charts—it would have made more sense to send the mother to counseling first, because dealing with her symptoms might automatically help her son. It was even possible that treating the child first would backfire. If the son in this example responded to counseling by talking more and starting to process his feelings, but the mother's symptoms went untreated, she'd have difficulty offering him support. That would be detrimental to both. But as the department was structured, there was no way to make these kinds of determinations.

Laura had also noticed that some of the more junior clinical workers on the children's team were judgmental of their clients' parents—especially the parents of special needs boys. Those parents sometimes appeared to be disconnected from their children. But Laura's son, Leo, has ADHD. Laura is not a survivor of domestic violence. She isn't triggered by memories of an abusive ex-partner. And yet she still knows what it feels like to want to run away from her own child—to be so overwhelmed, from time to time, that she herself has to fight the urge to dissociate. Like her agency's clients, she has been judged for her parenting. Drawing on her own experience as a mother, Laura felt that pushing parents to do more would not necessarily build attachment; it would simply make the parents feel more defeated. Parents like that weren't asking for more assignments; they were asking for more empathy.

All in all, Laura saw that her department needed tools to measure progress. The staff needed to be trained in those tools. And in order to ensure that therapies were working across the board at the family level, Laura would need to integrate the teams within her department.

Some of the funding would come from the board; it stood

to reason that the programs Laura had set out to implement would be more efficient than the programs the agency had in place at that time. The agency's director, Judy Harris Kluger, had spent twenty-five years as a New York State judge. She was whip-smart and tenacious and had already become a strong ally. To secure the rest of the funding, Laura came up with a plan called the FamilySafe Project and turned to the Manhattan District Attorney's Office for funding. The DA had hundreds of millions of dollars of forfeiture funds. Through its Criminal Justice Investment Initiative, it distributed some of those funds to community organizations dedicated to decreasing violence. Laura secured a grant from the initiative and used it to solve several problems at once.

Developed by the adult and children's teams in unison with the additional support of family counselors, the FamilySafe assessment was an evidence-based screening tool designed to identify trauma, strengths, and supports. It also identified symptoms such as the extent of attachment disruption between children and parents who had been abused, but were not themselves abusive.

Sanctuary's clinicians were trained in several evidence-based treatments: trauma-focused cognitive behavioral therapy (TF-CBT), a highly structured, parent-child intervention that is considered best practice in the field of child abuse treatment; child-parent psychotherapy (CPP), which is the most effective evidence-based model for treating children aged five and under; and cognitive processing therapy (CPT), a time-limited effective treatment for PTSD that was originally developed for survivors of sexual assault. The FamilySafe assessment would help clinicians decide on the model that would be most effective with each client. It would provide concrete metrics that allowed clinicians to determine whether and when clients needed more services. And it would force teams within the department to work together and treat families as indivisible units. (To help ensure that they did so, Laura also implemented a weekly meeting in which both tracks were encouraged to discuss cases and intakes holistically.)

Even by social work standards, none of this was glamorous. But it was crucial and, as the metrics soon showed, effective. Now, whenever a client walked through the agency's doors, a social worker told them that Sanctuary worked with the entire family. They were told that they would be assessed, that Sanctuary would examine the results, and that the family as a whole would receive the services they required. Within the agency this represented a sea change in thinking, and that change continued to pay dividends. Having measurement systems in place made it easier for Sanctuary to raise more funds: there were concrete numbers that its development people could point to. On the case-by-case level, those same numbers showed Sanctuary's clinicians that, however traumatized their clients had been upon arrival, they did respond to treatment over time. For Laura's staff, that was profoundly validating, and in the boardroom it did not go unnoticed that the agency had proven itself capable of adapting when needs were going unmet.

"When I first got to Sanctuary," Laura says, "there was a resistance to change. I felt it.

"People would say, 'We do it the Sanctuary way.' Now people are much more open and excited about training and finding new ways to work—and that's exciting to me, because you don't just change and say, 'Okay, I'm done.' You have to *keep* changing."

SANCTUARY STAFF MEMBERS WHO work directly with clients speak more than thirty languages. Within Laura's department, licensed master's-level social workers speak more than fifteen. But in Queens, New York City's most diverse borough, you'll find speakers of 138 languages living side by side. Every one of those languages represents a culture with its own norms and values, which Sanctuary's clinicians take into account whenever they work with a client. Given the work that the agency does and the communities it serves, cultural sensitivity is critical—and while Sanctuary has always been deeply progressive, it has its own organizational baggage, its own institutional biases. And so by the time the murders of George Floyd, Breonna Taylor, and Ahmaud Arbery brought systemic injustice to the forefront of a national conversation on race, the agency's staff had already committed itself to a program of rooting those biases out, exploring its own practices, and pinpointing microaggressions. The program was called Diversity, Equity, and Inclusion, or DEI. Laura's clinical staff met and posed a series of questions, including: What could they do to make Sanctuary an anti-racist agency? What did they need to do to live up to that ideal?

In a DEI meeting for her staff members there was a general airing of grievances and frustrations. Some wanted more transparency and better communication—a clearer sense of how decisions were made. There were concerns about the way men were viewed: Were gay couples being treated differently? Were questions being posed in a way that suggested the agency didn't believe male survivors? Other staff members talked about opportunities that seemed slanted in favor of clinicians. Why did they seem to get all the training even though case managers had more direct contact with clients?

"People were angry," Laura recalls. "They were disgruntled. We held a senior staff meeting and talked about the challenge of not being defensive. We had to listen. We had to think about what we were hearing. We had to push ourselves to be better."

Laura had the most diverse department within the agency, but there were obvious areas in need of improvement, starting with recruitment and internships. The previous director of clinical services had recruited from Columbia University, which tends to have more white students. Laura recruited more from Hunter College and Fordham University. She was looking for a wide range of life experiences: people who were single parents, or had been raised by single parents, or had grown up translating for immigrant parents. In job interviews, prospective clinicians were asked, "What is your understanding of anti-racist practices?" and "What is your sense of your own privilege?"

"Some people just did not get it," Laura says. "But having had an education is a privilege. Having legal status is a privilege. We were trying to attract people who'd done that thinking before coming to us. When someone said, 'I don't see color' or 'I try to be really nice,' that's not what we're looking for. I want you to have really thought about it, especially if you're white. How can you do social work *without* thinking about it? Everyone here knows that 'cultural competence' is a trigger with me. You can't be 'competent' in someone else's culture. I prefer cultural humility: a desire to understand someone else's culture so that you can help them on their terms, not on yours."

Laura recalls a client who came in with three boys, all of whom had learning and behavioral issues. Clinicians on the children's team wanted this mother to have heartfelt conversations with her sons—to become clued in to their struggles. As far as they were concerned, she was disassociating and not connecting. But on at least one occasion the boys had gotten into fights in the waiting room that were so serious that male staffers were called in to intervene. As far as Laura was concerned, it was no wonder the mother wasn't connecting. In this woman's culture, kids were raised communally. Grandparents were involved. The whole village helped. Now the mother was in a shelter by herself with three boys who were out of control. It made perfect sense that she wanted to run. The children's team wanted to schedule three back-to-back sessions—one for each child's therapist—to tell the client about all the things she'd done wrong. But Laura couldn't imagine a more torturous scenario than for a client to be told in three consecutive sessions about all the ways she was failing her children. Laura told the clinicians, "You are asking her for something she can't give right now. You want her to be present in a way she can't be."

Another mother, who had enrolled in Sanctuary's Economic Empowerment Program, would drop her kid off in agency day care. This child was difficult, too—the first few days were a disaster—and some staff members judged the woman for not phasing her child in over the course of two weeks. When Laura saw that she thought, *Have you been parents? Working parents* have *to drop their children off.*

"Clinicians were bringing their middle-class views of parenting into the room," Laura recalls. "Like, 'Parents should be emotionally available.' But some cultures are less open to being outwardly emotional in front of strangers than others. Assuming your parenting style is the best and that people should aspire to parent your way, that ties in a little bit to white supremacy—the idea that you have set the standard for parenting and everyone has to come to your place of parenting."

LAURA EMBRACED DEI IMMEDIATELY, not only because the program aligned with her own core beliefs, but because it aligned with her experience as a Latina woman. Laura's maternal grandmother, a Midwestern WASP, had been a teacher at Hull House—as progressive an organization as America has ever produced. And yet, when Laura's mother, Margaret, married Laura's father, Rafael, the family took charge of Margaret's money, so that Rafael—a Cuban immigrant—could not steal it.

"We didn't have a name for microaggressions back then," Laura says, "but my father encountered many of them. People talked about his manners, his accent. He came here with nothing and ended up with a doctorate from the University of Chicago but still had to fight to be accepted. My father was fluent in French and English as well as Spanish, and knew a good bit of German, as well. But when he got here he was told, 'You should get a job at a gas station.'"

Rafael ended up working in settings that Laura remembers as very WASPy and very reserved.

"He was seen as too loud, as too much," she says. "When I was little, we lived in Lake Forest, in Illinois. My father was a professor of art history, working on his PhD, and it was an idyllic life: kids frolicking in the backyards and the front doors always open. We were happy. But he didn't get tenure. It was a big blow. He had been accused of sexism. Part of that may have been because he had a very expressive Latino personality. And I wonder now if being a Latino man and having mostly white students played a role."

Rafael and Margaret moved to western Massachusetts, where Rafael became a curator of prints and drawings at the Clark Art Institute and taught art history at Williams College. "My mother had a horrible time," Laura recalls.

"She had left a community where everyone was open and friendly and landed in a community where we'd be seen as newcomers for twenty-five years. In Williamstown, people were formal. The house next door had girls my age, but I was never invited over. I wasn't invited to a birthday party and found out it was because people thought that my laugh was too loud. Eventually, things did improve. My mother got a job at a school as an art teacher. She began to make friends and found her own creative outlets. In the long run it turned out to be the better community. It was outdoorsy. Every summer I worked with my father at the Clark. We built a good life. But, of course, it was very white, and we were still seen as exotic. We were 'the Fernandezes.' My father had an accent. Life was different for us. We were always talking about different things than my friends were."

Laura remembers that Rafael would get upset if an everyday object went missing.

"Why is he so upset?" she'd ask her mother.

"He lost a country," Margaret would say, and Laura would think, *How do you lose a country?*

In sixth grade, Laura read *On the Beach*, a novel about nuclear apocalypse. The year before, her teachers had intimated that nuclear war was inevitable and that everyone would die in a nuclear winter. But Laura's sixth-grade teacher took the opposite tack.

"It's *not* inevitable," that teacher said. "We're reading this book because we *can* make a difference. We can organize. We can stop things. We can change the world."

This struck a chord, sparking Laura's lifelong interest in politics. In college she became obsessed with Latin American history and the way countries like Cuba had gone from repressive regimes run by the rich to repressive regimes run by Communists. How did that happen? Was there a way to advocate for human rights without having to give up human freedoms?

Laura was thirty when Rafael passed away. "He had prostate cancer and untreated sleep apnea, which killed him," she says. "But I think it was also exhaustion. Leaving a country and all the loss that entailed. A lot of people in his position became alcoholics: you pay a price when you leave and start over. He was always trying to prove he belonged."

As a child, Laura had known two distinct, disparate worldviews: Margret's and Rafael's. Consequently she knew there were many more worldviews out there and felt comfortable in a variety of settings.

"I'm not fully a person of color," she says today. "But I'm not a person who's full of white privilege. And, you know, my Cuban family's worldview is also unique to them: it's not like there's one Cuban way of being. It's how your family lives its values. So I was glad to see DEI come along. I was already interested in hearing about—and being open to—our clients' values and the way they live their culture."

WHEN IT CAME TO the struggle against racism and structural inequality, Sanctuary had been forward-thinking. But COVID-19 caught all of New York by surprise. A week before lockdown, Laura's clinicians came to her and asked if they should cancel group sessions.

"Keep going," Laura told them. "Everyone, finish your groups."

The next day she canceled the groups.

"What's happening?" Laura's deputy asked her. "You just told everyone to keep going."

"That was yesterday," Laura replied.

Even so, it took a few days for the reality to sink in. At first there was a sense that COVID-19 was "just a virus"—

that the agency could just push through. Laura's boss Judy was scheduled to go to a state meeting in Albany; Laura and the staff had to remind her of the health risks. They pleaded with her not to go. Gradually, the realization sunk in: COVID-19 was going to be different from any challenge they had encountered.

As a lockdown grew closer, everyone understood that incidents of domestic violence were going to rise. There was no question that Sanctuary's shelters were going to stay open. But in Laura's nonresidential programs matters were not quite so clear-cut. How was she going to weigh the safety of her staff against the safety of her clients? The clients had never been more vulnerable. The social workers had martyrdom embedded in their DNA. Telling them to stay home would not be so easy.

On Tuesday, March 10, 2020—five days before New York City closed its schools—Laura started canceling clinical meetings. She also canceled residential meetings and non-essential travel. Staff members were told to ask themselves three questions before coming to work:

Have I had contact with anyone who might be infected?
Have I traveled anywhere?
Do I have a fever?

At the shelters, directors came up with a plan in which two managers would stay on site while everyone else worked from home. At the agency's headquarters, Laura had everyone on staff call and check in with every one of their clients.

"Initially, we weren't even thinking about getting our telehealth platform up and running," she recalls. "We were in crisis mode. Were our clients safe? Did they have the resources they needed? Did we have a safe way to reach them? People were communicating in any way that they could: FaceTime, Google Voice, Zoom—whatever they could find that worked. Later on, staff members said that they hadn't received direction. *I* had no direction! It was all so overwhelming. The immediate fear was that our clients were going to be stuck with their abusers. But we worried about the staff's safety, too."

Thursday, March 12, was Laura's last day in the office, but she didn't know it at the time. She met with senior staff that afternoon to discuss a new grant. She started a plan to transition the clients of a clinician who was about to resign. It was intern season, so she matched interns with clients. Earlier, on Monday, at a training for the interns, Laura had told them, "I've lived through a lot of crises.

This is going to be another crisis, but New York's resilient. We're going to be fine." Now she wasn't feeling so sure. An intern who had started her field placement that January had come from China. That intern was fearful now for her country, and for herself: on the streets of the city, a certain amount of violence was being directed at Asians.

On Friday, Laura and her son Leo were due to fly to a family wedding in Florida.

"Should I come?" she had asked her cousin.

"You should come," the cousin had said.

Laura was nervous. She didn't want to be responsible for bringing the virus across state lines. She was worried about her family, too: "Cubans are very kissy," she says. "I had to be, like, 'Don't touch me!' But Florida was fascinating. The TVs all seemed to be playing Fox News. Everyone seemed to think COVID-19 was a hoax."

"We got through the wedding, but I was so stressed the whole time," Laura says. "I had impending doom on my mind with the virus, and work, and what if I'm sick? On Sunday, I had to check out of my hotel and go to my cousin's house to wait for my flight. I was looking at her clock but it hadn't been changed over for daylight savings. I barely made it to the airport. I was panicking by that point, thinking, *I need to get out of here. I need to get to my house, isolate, figure out work.* Leo and I had to bolt for the gate. We ran and when we got on the plane we were sweating. We looked sick but we had made it."

On Monday, in her apartment in Brooklyn, Laura put Leo in front of a screen and went into her bedroom to work. People were posting about doing yoga and baking bread. *Who* are *these people?* Laura wondered. Laura hadn't showered. She practically threw food at Leo—hot dogs, mac and cheese. That night she fell into exhausted, nightmarish sleep.

"The first week was brutally stressful—different from my days in child welfare, when the stress involved clients and work," she recalls. "This was our own fear and stress. In normal times, if I was worried about work, I'd put a million hours in at the office. Now I was trapped at home, trying to make my computer work. That felt very different. We didn't have tools. We were having constant meetings, trying to figure out who needs what kind of equipment. How do we get calls forwarded? Our office manager went into the building and fixed that. But there was so much and it all had to happen so quickly."

Overnight, tiny things became big headaches. Sanctuary received its mail at the post office box shown on its website. Who was going to pick up the mail now? Who was going to open it, and where? That was an administrative problem and a legal problem on top of the logistics involved—and there were dozens of problems just like it. At one of the shelters a client threatened her roommate and coughed on a resident manager, saying she had COVID-19 and that the manager was going to get it, too. The manager was traumatized. The client was told she posed a safety risk and would have to move out of the shelter. In normal times, Sanctuary staffers might call the police to help with an eviction. Now the police showed up but refused to help. This had never happened before. It took several nerve-racking days before Sanctuary managed to get the city to move the client to another shelter.

"Everything felt so much harder than it had been, every decision that we had to make," Laura says. "And I was in Brooklyn, in my tiny apartment. I live near a hospital; the sirens were going all the time and we were still some weeks away from the top of the curve. I had a childcare provider who'd come in on snow days or if my son was sick, but her asthma made her high-risk, so I couldn't have her watch my child. On top of everything else, I felt trapped."

Laura obsessed over the plants in her office. She felt that they were symbolic—that everything around her was going to die. She was terrified for her city: for its essential workers, for the staff in her agency's shelters, for all the low-paid service workers who could not afford to stay home. *I'm sitting here while they're getting up, riding the subway, and going to work*, Laura thought. When a member of her staff got the plants and drove them out to Brooklyn, Laura felt relieved. But that did not make her feel any less guilty.

SOCIAL WORKERS ARE TRAINED to deal with crises: simple crises, sudden crises, creeping crises, complex crises, life-threatening crises. At one point or another, every social worker has to manage multiple, simultaneous crises. But this was the first time in living memory that everyone involved in a situation—social workers and clients alike— were experiencing the same crisis at the same time. There was no road map, no training, no clear way through. Still, Laura put on her bravest face.

I will lead my people through this, she told herself.

Laura imagined that she was being well organized, communicative, and decisive. But in reality she was none of those things. She was in shock. Two weeks into the lockdown, Laura's sister called from Williamstown and said, "Come home. You're overwhelmed. You need more support. You need another adult in the home, and more space."

By now the parents on Laura's staff were struggling. Some had quiet places to Zoom from, but many more had screaming kids in the background. Laura sent out messages that said, "I'm stressed. We're all stressed. I don't have the answer just yet." But her coworkers were thrilled when she finally left town. "Oh my god, I was worried about you!" they told her.

That was when Laura realized she hadn't been faking so well.

Up in Williamstown, with her mother and sister, Laura continued to work. A friend of hers—a pediatrician who was also raising a child on her own—had asked Laura to take the child in the event of her death. That was frightening: it was sobering to see a friend, who was also a doctor, write her will and sketch out worst-case scenarios. But what if Laura herself got exposed and became sick? Who would take care of Leo?

The economy scared Laura, too. No one she knew was spending money—there wasn't too much to spend money on, anyway—so what was going to happen to the stock market? What would happen to America's tax base? What would happen to New York's tax base if everyone fled the city and never came back? The list of what-ifs grew longer and longer. What would happen to Laura's staff and their clients if Sanctuary had to make massive cuts? The agency's annual fundraising gala took place every June and raised $2 million. Seth Meyers was set to host at Chelsea Piers—Seth's wife, Alexi, was one of the agency's lawyers—but how could the agency have a gala now? And what would happen if it didn't?

Closer to home, Laura worried about her staff. All over the city, Sanctuary's clients were suffering. What could she do to help her staff manage their feelings about it? In child welfare, Laura had been consumed by fears for her clients. It had taken her two years to learn how to put that worrying part of herself in a box. But Laura's junior staff members hadn't gone through that process. They didn't have the same boxes.

On a more practical level, there were endless hassles involving forms and receipts.

Even in the best of times, social work can be a daily grind of minutiae, a constant juggling of bureaucratic details. Now

Laura found herself building the plane she was flying—except the plane also seemed to be exploding. The systems she still had to navigate were convulsing, if not collapsing. But in spite of the shocks—or because of them—the same level of attention to detail was being demanded. On an individual level there comes a time when a social worker will skirt their own agency's policies, take a twenty-dollar bill out of her own wallet, and just pay for what needs to be paid for: a sandwich; a MetroCard; a new pair of shoes. But that wasn't something that Laura could do at an agencywide level, and in real time her clients were suffering.

Sanctuary had secured an emergency grant from the city to get gift cards for food and other essentials to clients. How would the agency distribute those gift cards? It couldn't ask clients to get on the subway to come to the office. The mail presented its own set of problems, especially for clients living with their abusers. On top of that, the city was asking for itemized receipts from clients. This was easier said than done. In theory, a client could have snapped pictures of their receipts on their phones. But in the real world, clients lost receipts, or spent the money they had on their gift cards over the course of several shopping trips, or wanted to save a certain amount for later. Sorting it all out was mind-numbing and infuriating: hours and hours of meetings went into trying, and failing, to solve the problem.

"Can't they accept that we just bought gift cards?" Laura asked. "Why do they need to be itemized? To me, it comes from the idea that clients might have been buying beer or luxury items—that we can't just trust them. But this is a pandemic. Are you kidding me?"

Other funders were more flexible. Laura spent a good deal of her time working with Sanctuary's development team, talking about different ways to show people that Sanctuary was still operating—that there were still compelling reasons to give. The agency never stopped operating at maximum capacity. But in April, when incidents of domestic violence spiked, the number of reports filed by the police went down. Partly this was because the city's police department was overwhelmed, too, with one-sixth of the force calling in sick. Some of the officers who stayed on duty refused to file reports or enforce orders of protection. But it also wasn't easy to call 911 when your abuser was next to you in the apartment.

Sanctuary set up a texting service—clients could duck into the bathroom and contact the agency silently—and there was a dramatic spike in clients seeking immediate help. But more work meant more paperwork, and Laura had to make sure that everyone got their notes in on time. "We need to prove we exist," she told her staff. "We need to *prove* we're doing the work."

At the same time, Sanctuary made sure that its staff members felt taken care of. For the first time in its history the agency implemented summer hours, making a point of acknowledging staff members' exhaustion. After all, if Sanctuary couldn't take care of the staff, how could its staff be expected to take care of clients? Gradually, piece by piece, problems were solved. Seth Meyers hosted a virtual gala from his apartment. Out of necessity, Laura's staff became accustomed to working from home. There were even a few silver linings: remote technology made therapy more accessible for clients, and because transportation was no longer an issue, fewer appointments were dropped. Laura wrapped her fiscal year up with no layoffs and no reductions in services offered to clients—although, by necessity, some of those services were now being offered online.

Laura dug in for the long haul in Massachusetts. She enrolled Leo in a local school. She accepted the fact that, for some unknowable period of time, she'd have to keep working remotely. But even at a remove she resolved to be present. One day, during an online all-staff meeting, she summarized the closing lines of a book called *Trauma Stewardship*.

"If we are going to do this work," she said, "we are going to bear witness to the world's suffering, and not every veteran will be healed—not every animal will be saved—but we can do the one thing we can do: be present for the world."

Laura wanted her staff to know that, even when they felt too tired to go on—when they felt helpless and useless—bearing witness to the pain of others was a radical act. "It takes a lot," she says. "People who aren't social workers might not understand just how taxing it is. But it opens you up to so much good stuff, too."

Resilience—the capacity for bouncing back from adversity—and resilience theory—the idea that the *kinds* of trauma people encounter is less important than the *manner* in which it is dealt with—are core concepts in social work, and the ability to identify and shore up resilience is a vital skill. Resilience is also a way for the social worker to view the client, not in terms of what they don't have, but in terms of what they *do* have. And a resilience-based approach does more than increase the client's ability to regain equilibrium; it helps the social worker look beyond the long list of challenges and difficulties that clients face and see all the things they can achieve. Laura and her staff were daily witnesses to violence, neglect, and poverty, but they also witnessed all that "good stuff": moments when clients who had been beaten down, brutalized, and threatened with deportation stood up again.

Ultimately, Laura and all of the members of her staff knew that they'd had a hand in supporting those transformations.

At Sanctuary for Families, there are clients who go on to be Survivor Leaders. Following a twelve-week training course, they become certified advocates who go out in the world and use their own stories to empower and encourage other survivors of domestic violence. Laura told us about one of those women, an undocumented immigrant who had COVID-19, recovered, and went out and got a job with the U.S. Census Bureau. Like all Survivor Leaders, she was the walking definition of resilience.

"She's thrilled, so glad to be working, but also thrilled to have found this very American job," Laura says. "I think about what this client went through—how much she had stacked against her—and here she is, so excited about the census. It's amazing, the things our clients can do."

2

JOHN BARR

The phones could have been ringing in Pleasant Plains on Staten Island, in Brownsville, Brooklyn, or in Riverdale in the Bronx. The phones rang five days a week, Monday through Friday, in rich neighborhoods and poor alike. The voice on the other end of the line said the same thing every time:

"My name is John Barr, and I'm calling from the medical examiner's office."

If you were hearing those words, it meant that someone close to you had died—very recently, more likely than not of a drug overdose. John Barr knew a bit about the circumstances. He had a folder full of facts and photographs, a full report drawn up by the medicolegal investigator (MLI) who'd been dispatched to examine the scene. But there was more information John needed to unearth, and nothing about that process was going to be easy.

"The person I'm calling is someone I found in the MLI's report," John tells us the first time we meet, at a Manhattan café a few blocks away from the Office of the Chief Medical Examiner (OCME), on East Twenty-Sixth Street in Manhattan. "What that means is the person I'm speaking with made the discovery, witnessed the death, or intends to claim the body if they haven't already. It could be the best friend, or a family member, or intimate partner of the deceased. It could be a sister or brother. Sometimes a grandparent. But more often than not, it's a parent: someone who's just had the worst day of his or her life—probably the worst day that they'll ever have. And now they're dealing with me."

John measures his words carefully, as he would on the phone. There are privacy issues to keep in mind as we speak, but there's more to his reticence than that. There is respect for the arc of a life and for all the bad turns and misfortunes that lead Americans to use drugs and die from them in ever-increasing numbers.

Long before the arrival of COVID-19, the United States was grappling with another epidemic. Over the course of twenty years, overdose rates in America had doubled and doubled again, going from 16,000 in 1999 to 70,999 in 2019—the first year in which more Americans died of accidental opioid overdoses than in car crashes. Every year newer, more power-ful synthetic drugs were killing tens of thousands of people, including functional users who'd been self-medicating for years, even decades. For two of those years, since he started with the OCME in 2018, John had tried to sort out the causes and bring these tragedies into close focus—to make sense of events that are routinely described as "senseless."

To do so, John interviewed those closest to the departed, methodically gathering the kind of data the MLI's reports can't possibly cover: Did the deceased have a history of trauma (specifically, childhood trauma)? Were they pre-scribed opiates for an injury or a surgery and not given the help they needed to get off of them, leading them to become overprescribed or leading them to street drugs they used to self-medicate? John was looking to unlock users' innermost secrets—to see the things these men and women took great pains to hide, not just from their loved ones but from them-selves. He was going after the most sensitive stuff there is, and his approach over the phone was as important as the information he was calling to convey.

"The person I'd called probably thought I was going tell them what the cause of death may have been," he explains. "But that's not something I'd know until the toxicology results came back, and that could take several weeks. So the next thing I'd say is 'I don't have any new information at this time.' Some of the people I was talking to were still in shock. Others understood immediately. They'd say, 'Oh, that's why I thought you were calling.' Or they'd say, 'How long do we have to wait?' The opportunity to explain the process was also my chance to establish the fact that I was there not to judge but to help. I'd answer every question that was posed to me. Only then would I say, 'I'm a social worker. I've been hired to investigate suspected drug overdoses. Is that something that you'd be able to talk about?'"

BEFORE THE OCME HIRED John, his position didn't exist. As far as he knew, there were no equivalent jobs anywhere. Medical examiners' offices across the country investigated deaths, and that's all that they did. They were staffed by forensic pathologists; they didn't employ social workers to work with the living. But for John the idea of going into uncharted territory was part of the draw—the notion of having a job he created as he went along, using his skills as a social worker to assess his work environment in the way that he might have assessed a client:

Where could he make a difference?

What resources did he lack to make that difference?

How could he improvise to make a difference anyway?

Typically, social workers who specialize in research go on to earn PhDs. They publish papers and often teach. But the work John was doing was not quite research, because it wasn't yet clear what the information he mined would be used for. Nor could his work be called direct practice—because all his clients were dead.

It was a unique position for a social worker to find himself in. "Fundamental to social work is attention to the environmental forces that create, contribute to, and address problems in living"—that's how the National Association of Social Workers put it in the preamble to their code of ethics. But for John's clients the problem in living was that they had died. And by taking on his role at the OCME, John sought to bring attention to the forces—the social determinants of health—that created and contributed to this problem.

In his cubicle, John had a phone with a headset, a desktop PC. On the shelf above his head he kept social work textbooks, books on death and dying, and the American Psychiatric Association's *Diagnostic and Statistical Manual of Mental Disorders, Fifth Edition*, or *DSM-5*. The only personal touch, aside from his lunch, was a copy of Vivian Gornick's writing manual *The Situation and the Story: The Art of Personal Narrative*. John consulted it while turning the interviews he had been conducting into prose narratives, taking the shards of broken lives he'd collected and turning them into portraits. Four times a year, at One Police Plaza—where the City of New York Police Department is headquartered—those narratives were read out loud, in bullet-point form, to a room full of top brass from the NYPD, representatives of DA's offices in all five boroughs, fire department officials, and administrators from various hospitals, the Department of Health, and the Department of Correction. Officials had high hopes for John's pilot program. At first, at least, it seemed as though the whole city were listening.

Another core value outlined in the social worker's code of ethics is the "dignity and worth of the person": "Social workers are cognizant of their dual responsibility to clients and to the broader society. They seek to resolve conflicts between clients' interests and the broader society's interests in a socially responsible manner consistent with the values, ethical principles, and ethical standards of the profession."

As a social work intern at Defender Services of Harlem—
a public defender's office in Upper Manhattan—John had
written reports on pre-pleading investigations to advocate for clients who might have been granted alternatives
to incarceration. These reports had been narratives, too,
highlighting problems in living that may have created or
contributed to an individual's decision to transgress against
social controls—they were much more than summaries of
infractions. At the OCME, John hoped that storytelling
would ensure that deaths weren't just written off as cases of
the deceased "getting what they deserved." That their lost
lives would be approached and seen in all their complexity.
And who better to speak to that complexity than the people
who loved John's decedents? Who, in many cases, had done
all they could have to try and save them?

John hoped that researchers and policy makers would
study these portraits, see the epidemic's true face, and gain
a firmer grasp of its root causes so they could better arm
themselves to combat it. At the time that was only a hope,
but hope enough to counter some of the sadness John found
himself processing in the course of doing his job.

"Some days," he says, "I just didn't have it in me. Here
I am, staring at dozens of cases and bodies, and it's no

different from the week before or the week before that. But now, for some reason, I just can't bear the thought of picking up the phone. There were days I took off and just wrote narratives. Then I'd remind myself that when I did call, tremendous amounts of positive energy came back at me. The pictures and the reports start to feel pretty unreal after a while, but that direct contact makes them feel concrete again. There's still a feeling of doubt and anticipation, at the outset. But, almost always, I end up feeling lifted and invigorated. The people on the other end of the line are so strong, it's remarkable."

John tended to get to the office by 8:30 in the morning. He caught up on his emails, worked on a narrative or two, then he logged on to the medical examiner's content management system and looked at the day's influx of cases, which interns had already divided into three categories:

One: Witnesses saw the deceased taking drugs.

Two: Drugs or drug paraphernalia were found at the scene.

Three: The MLI report mentions a history of drug use but no drugs or drug paraphernalia were found at the scene.

Mondays were especially heavy because interns didn't work on the weekends—the cases piled up—and because deaths tended to spike between Friday and Sunday. Sometimes there were a dozen cases. Sometimes there were more.

John almost always made calls regarding the ones and twos: cases in which the decedent had been seen using drugs or drug paraphernalia had been found at the scene. Threes tended to be trickier. Circumstantially, they were unclear. *Something* had happened to the deceased. They didn't fall off of a building. There was no blunt trauma involved. The cause of death could have been a heart attack, a stroke, an embolism. But there were signs of drug overdoses that John had learned to look out for: Had the deceased been found kneeling—for instance, in a prayer position? Was the room they were found in dirty or in disarray? Basement apartments were a telltale sign, too. After a while you developed a sixth sense, and more often than not John's hunches panned out. But whether or not he was going to be making a call, John studied every case closely and searched for patterns. He had learned to expect spikes in July and August: more people are out and about in the warmer months; it's easier to buy drugs; more hand-to-hand sales might have been happening. In his two years on the job, John watched fentanyl go from being *a* problem to being *the* problem. He saw toxicology reports where fentanyl was present give way to reports where fentanyl was the *only* drug present. Fentanyl is cheaper than heroin. And, unlike heroin, fentanyl is always around.

An old-timer told John in 2019, "You know, sometimes there wouldn't be any stuff. You couldn't get anything anywhere. But now there's always someone who's selling."

If there was always somebody selling, there was always somebody buying. If there was always somebody buying, there was always going to be a reason for John Barr to pick up the phone. In 2019 the death rate did not dip when summer ended, as it usually does. John likened the phenomenon to global warming: "We just had the hottest months of the year over, and over, and over again. The end of 2019 and the start of the following year was unprecedented."

ON MOST DAYS, at ten in the morning, John picked up the phone and made his first call of the day.

Almost without exception, the people he reached were

willing to talk—if only because they viewed John as an extension of law enforcement. "Sometimes, I'd get perfunctory answers," he says. "That happened quite a bit, actually, and it's a weird area, ethically, because I *was* calling to investigate a death, and these people felt beholden to the process. When that happened, it wasn't an explicit refusal to speak to me. But effectively, it was a refusal."

In cases like that, John kept talking. He kept on asking questions. He made sure that the person he was talking to knew he could be of use to them. If he hadn't already given them his phone number, he'd do it now and encourage them to call anytime. In John's experience, people softened up when a service was being offered.

"I won't pretend it's not strenuous work," he says. "Talking to people under these circumstances . . . at best, it's emotionally exhausting for them as well as for me. That's a given, a bad place to be. I just try to go there with the people that I'm talking to. It's not empathy, even, so much as a willingness to be overwhelmed. To feel my way through this devastating situation that's also devastatingly human, while maintaining the ability to do my job."

Sometimes the person John called claimed not to know anything: *He was a grown-up; I didn't ask about his business.*

"But they might have known more than they thought they did," John explains. "For instance, they might be imagining I want to know what happened on the night of the death—who their deceased relative was with, what they were up to, and so forth—whereas what I'm looking for is actually much more open-ended. I'm not trying to build a case. The district attorney (who paid my salary), the medical examiner (who created my position), and the drug traffic investigators (who hired me) were all looking for certain kinds of information. But I would start from a social worker's perspective—and the crucial thing there to get across is whatever happened to the deceased person was not their fault. Sometimes, when the mother or father or brother or sister says, 'I don't know anything,' what they're really saying is 'I don't want to speak ill.'"

In practice, the shame and the stigma attached to drug use was a constant obstacle John had to contend with. More times than he can count, he heard parents pray for a negative tox screen—even parents who *knew* that their children were using. The burden of guilt was palpable: even over a telephone line, it was almost a physical presence. Still, John had to move forward and get as much data as he could. So he'd pry gently:

Do you know if they ever used?

Was there something in the past that you knew about?

"It's natural to evade, initially," he says. "But the thing is, I don't care if they knew. That's what I try to get at. A lot of people don't realize the way these parents have been punished and beaten up by their peers: 'You should have kicked him out a long time ago!' But how are you going to give up on your kid? Sometimes parents do turn a blind eye. But who are the neighbors to judge? Yes, people make decisions in their lives. But in terms of what gets somebody on the losing end of a syringe? That's extreme. It's almost like saying, 'They got what they deserved,' and now they're saying it to the parents, too."

Then again, the shame that a parent feels may stem from the fact that they truly didn't know or weren't able to admit to themselves that their child was using. And in cases like that, it's often shame that is resting on shame that their child would have felt.

Here's what that dynamic might look like:

A daughter lies to her father because she's embarrassed about her drug use. But the shame she feels about lying only exacerbates the pain that caused her to turn to substances in the first place. The daughter's desperate not to lie, but she does—and there's a good chance the father believes her, because he's just as desperate to avoid the truth.

In John's experience, this dynamic played out again and again, in family after family. Here's what it looked like, written up in one of his narratives:

> The decedent's grandmother believes that her
> grandson, who lived at home, was "always so
> stressed and nervous" because he was manag-
> ing her expectations. Although he knew she
> "would never abandon him," he was ashamed
> of his substance use and needed her approval.
> Over the years she spent "$200,000, at least,
> to keep him afloat." Even so, he "lashed out"
> repeatedly, because she would not give him
> money, telling her he could not wait for her
> to die so he could collect the insurance pay-
> ment. He apologized each time and contin-
> ued lying to her about his use. "Tell parents to
> stop looking for signs and symptoms of abuse.
> Tell them to look for signs of a double life."
> The decedent lied because he didn't want
> to disappoint his grandmother. She believed

his lies because she did not want to be disappointed.

This was concrete information and therefore useful. The grandmother's hard-earned advice was worth heeding. But it did not get to the root of the problem: the "original trauma" (in social work–speak) that drove the departed to use and misuse substances in the first place. Sometimes it really was something as simple as surgery: Sally crashes her motorcycle, crushes her hip, spends two months in the hospital, and gets hooked on prescription pain pills. When the prescription runs out, she turns to street drugs. But time and again John found himself looking for clues buried in the past: a history of sexual abuse, domestic violence, abandonment, or neglect, among a host of other factors.

The true cause of death wasn't just something that happened five minutes before the decedent's heart ceased to beat. It might have been something that happened five years ago—or fifty.

When it came to childhood trauma, a good deal depended on who was doing the talking. Sometimes parents did offer things up, depending on whether it involved them directly. Perhaps there was a spouse or a former spouse they no longer felt obliged to protect. John might have asked something as simple as *What were they like when they were young?* or *Did they have any struggles as a young person?* Some people would talk about those things and others would not, but John found that brothers and sisters were more willing to talk. Younger people understood in ways that their parents may have not that things that happen to children resonate into adulthood.

Even so, John would still hear: *Nope. All normal.*

In those cases, he might have asked something along the lines of *Did they finish high school?*

He found that persistence paid off. Maybe the decedent *did* drop out of high school—but again, John didn't judge. *Maybe that's a common thing*, he'd tell himself. *Maybe everyone in that neighborhood dropped out of high school.*

At the same time certain facts did raise the odds of certain outcomes.

The police saw drug overdose and thought *Social Darwinism*, or viewed the problem in terms of distribution and the evils of drug trafficking. Harm reduction advocates focused on systemic change: clean needles, safe injection sites, messaging, and medication. But John's interpretation of the social work perspective—"the ecological systems approach

of person-in-context"—meant that nothing that a decedent's loved one could tell him was irrelevant to his line of
questioning. This led him to ask questions that no one else
might have asked:

Did they have children?

When was the last time they saw their kids?

When John found out that a decedent had lost her paren-
tal rights and been denied visitation, that went some ways
toward answering the broader question of why she might
have been risking, or seeking, oblivion.

Case by case, as he grew into the job, John's array of
questions and strategies developed.

JOHN IS FORTY-SEVEN BUT trim as he was at the age of
sixteen, with dark, soulful eyes, a black beard, and a full
head of thick, wiry hair that started to gray when he was
fresh out of college and working as an apprentice video editor in Manhattan. *You've Got Mail*, the rom-com with Tom
Hanks and Meg Ryan, was one of the first films that he
worked on after graduating from Bennington. But John's
own tastes were much more esoteric—he liked foreign films
and old silent movies; he spent most of his spare hours in

New York's art house theaters—and much as he liked his coworkers, he became increasingly frustrated with the work itself. After a few years he quit and signed up to be a schoolteacher in rural Virginia. This was a soul-crushing job in the middle of soul-crushing poverty. He stayed up late to work on his lessons, but nothing he did in the classroom seemed to make a difference. And so, he returned to New York and bounced between jobs. He drank too much, too, and misused drugs on occasion—the hard stuff, though he kept that under wraps.

John had a gift, it turned out, for compartmentalizing his own double life. He had friends scattered all over the place, and he was always driving out of the city to visit them, but they didn't necessarily know about each other, and none of them knew more about John than he wanted them to. There were a couple of old friends from college that he used drugs with: a man named Andrew who lived in the country, a day's drive away, and a woman named Jen who'd driven down from Vermont with John the first time he visited Manhattan, and bought heroin with him in Alphabet City. Physically, he remained fit—Andrew and Jen were discreet—and John's secrets stayed hidden. But financially, he was on shaky ground, and in other ways he was lost. John didn't like being told what to do. And yet, before long he found himself wishing someone would come along and do just that.

In the meantime America had launched its invasions of Afghanistan and Iraq. John's father had been in Air Force ROTC in college and volunteered to be an Army infantry officer in Vietnam. His grandfather had flown in the Pacific in the Army Air Corps and retired from the Air Force as a colonel. John felt torn. On the one hand, he opposed the invasions. On the other, he felt compelled to serve—and, again, the thought of letting someone else make all the decisions was appealing.

One day he walked from his apartment in Astoria, Queens, to a recruiting station in Queensborough Plaza and enlisted as a medic in the Army. "I thought I could help," he recalls. "I wasn't a run-of-the-mill Army recruit. I didn't know too many Bennington grads who had joined the armed forces. But I also believed that, if someone like me wasn't willing to serve, what right did I have to criticize those who were? I ended up being deployed to Afghanistan. First I was in Kandahar. From there I went to Forward Operating Base Salerno. Then I was at Bagram Airfield. I served my second tour in Iraq, at Camp Victory outside of Baghdad."

At thirty-four—the age at which he'd gone into the Army—John was at least a decade older than most of the soldiers he served with. While they played video games and worked out, he read books. When they ran around in the barracks, swatting each other with towels, he sat in his bunk and tried to make sense of where he was and how he had gotten there. His thoughts would turn to his kid sister, Megan, who had been born with Down syndrome; of the shame his parents felt over having a disabled child; of the way he'd stepped in, at an early age, to become her primary caregiver; of the guilt he felt over having left her when he'd gone off to college.

"I found that I have an affinity for people we tend to think of as castoffs, if we think of them at all—the people we'd rather not see," John says. "Being in the Army expanded my vision. I began to recognize the many different kinds of people who had gone unseen by me, and by everyone else. Once I saw that, I couldn't stop seeing it. I couldn't stop wanting more from myself and from everyone else."

John didn't know at the time that he was being pulled toward social work. When his tours of duty were over, he took advantage of the G.I. Bill and enrolled in the master's program in Eastern classics at St. John's College's Santa Fe, New Mexico, campus.

"I didn't know what I wanted to get out of it," John recalls, but the program turned out to be a good fit. Over nine months he traced the course of the Buddha and his teachings from India to Japan. He learned about bodhisattvas—enlightened ones who were capable of reaching Nirvana but chose to stay in the world in order to alleviate the sufferings of others. All the while, he thought, *Wow, this is clicking.* For the first time John's weird trajectory from video editing to the Army—where he'd realized not only that he was good at helping people but that he liked doing so—was starting to make sense.

"Because I was older when I went into the Army, I ended up taking care of everyone around me," he says. "I took care of the patients. I took care of the other medics. I started to see my connection to people who'd defined their lives in terms of service. Grad school helped me put that into perspective; in that sense, it was good timing. But it was also a terrible time because my friend Jen died of a drug overdose in Massachusetts while I was living in New Mexico. She'd been sober for seven years and then she started using again."

Everything that John's friend Jen had done after college had been an effort to quit using drugs. For a very long time all those efforts had failed. Then there was a terrible car accident in which Jen's boyfriend died. She had been driving and using that day, and when she'd recovered enough physically, John drove her to court. To avoid going to prison, Jen pled no contest to vehicular homicide charges and agreed to go into treatment. But before finishing she went into Boston to score. She got busted and, because she had violated the terms of her probation, was sentenced to eighteen months in prison.

After serving her time, Jen stayed sober. Years passed, and then she moved from Cape Cod, where she had been living, to her brother's town. Her brother had a child and was separated from his wife, and Jen moved out there to help. "She was over the moon for that kid," John says, "but when her brother reconciled with his wife, the wife forbade Jen from seeing the child. That was part of the deal that they had, but it broke Jen's heart. She went back to Cape Cod, moved in with her sponsor, who had become a close friend, and was living in the sponsor's basement. But the despair got to be too much for her."

When the sponsor discovered that Jen was using again it did not end the friendship, but Jen had to move out of the house. The last time John talked to her, six months before he found out she had died, she reached out and told him about another car accident she had gotten into. Jen couldn't afford to get the car fixed, she said, and John lent her a thousand dollars. When he asked her via text if she was using again, she denied it.

"Except for the fact that she happened to die in Cape Cod, it was no different from any of the cases that cross my desk at the medical examiner's office," he says.

JOHN HAD LONG SINCE stopped misusing opiates. He didn't think he'd ever use them again. He barely drank anymore. But he did use hallucinogens on occasion, and hallucinogens were the thing that finally led him to social work. Passing through Clackamas County, in Oregon, on the way to another friend's place in Portland, John was pulled over by a state policeman who had noticed his out-of-state license plates. When the trooper leaned in for a look, he saw a Ziploc bag full of psychedelic mushrooms lying out in the open.

John had had time to cover them up. He could have swept them under the seat. But he'd been on the road for a long time and didn't think anything of it.

"Can I help you, Officer?" he said.

In retrospect, getting arrested that day was one of the best things that had ever happened to John.

"I decided to become a social worker while I was in jail up in Oregon," he says. "It was because of the people I had been locked up with. Most of them were 'frequent flyers': they'd get arrested for minor drug offenses, spend the night, get released, get arrested again. We were in a cell that was the size of a suburban bedroom and that cell was packed. There were thirty of us, maybe more, standing, sitting, talking a mile a minute. I had my eye on one guy. He wasn't jittery like the other prisoners. There was something about him. I said, 'What's going on, man? You don't look like someone who just got arrested.' It turned out, he hadn't been. He had actually been in for sixty days, for larceny, and was processing out.

"He and his girlfriend had gotten high on meth, gone to a store, and tried to steal a laptop or something equally stupid," John continues. "But his story was especially sad because he had eight other felonies for dumb things he'd done high on meth. At the same time he'd been clean for close to ten years. Not coincidentally, it had been a decade since he'd last been arrested. What that meant was he was on the verge of having all those old felonies expunged. In the course of those ten years, he and his girlfriend had had a child—a girl, who was now nine years old. She had become a ward of the state, with him and his girlfriend in jail.

"The guy was full of regret. He was also convinced that he could put his life back together, given the chance. I don't know if he needed advocacy or just encouragement. I don't know that anyone he had in his life could have filled either role. But I was there then to say, 'Okay. Here's what you have to do: you need to get your daughter back. In order to do that, you have to stay sober. And if your girlfriend is using, you do whatever you need to steer clear of her.'

"I learned later on in social work school that you're not supposed to give advice. You're supposed to help the person articulate their own response to the problem. But this guy was scared, obviously. Aside from his daughter, his girlfriend was the most important person in his life. He didn't know how he was going to negotiate that. And in the course of talking him through it, I realized that there was a place in that setting for someone like me: someone qualified to speak to the people that I was in with, understand how they had come to be there, and help them navigate this complex, bureaucratic system—which is what the Army had been.

"The more I talked to the people in that cell, trying to break them out of these cycles they'd found themselves in, the more I found myself filling that role," John says.

LATER THAT YEAR JOHN applied and was accepted into the social work program at Fordham University, on Manhattan's Upper West Side. He took classes in research methods, human development, and social work practice, and started his first-year internship at the Neighborhood Defender Service of Harlem. The office, on Lenox Avenue just north of 125th Street, was full of investigators; immigration, family law, and civil attorneys; and public defenders. All of them were overwhelmed by their caseloads, but John's supervisor, who was also a Bennington grad, took the time to give him a wide range of cases. Sometimes all he did was show up in court. "If there's a middle-aged white man in the audience who can be identified as a support person, that alone can make a difference," John says. Sometimes he did more, helping his clients into work programs that kept them off of the streets and strengthened their cases in court. He wrote reports on pre-pleading investigations, which put whatever actions had gotten his clients in trouble into perspective. He talked to parents, employers, and teachers, and wrote about childhood abuse, neglect, and malnutrition, lack of educational opportunities in the past, poor living conditions in the present, homelessness—the ABC's of poverty—in hopes of swaying the courts to be more lenient. He worked with people accused of low-level drug offenses, burglary, and child abuse. One of his clients had violated parole by jumping a turnstile. But not all of his clients welcomed the help.

"There was one guy who'd been arrested for possession of cocaine," John recalls. "The extenuating circumstance in that case was his wife had recently died. The two of them had met in recovery and gotten sober together; you could see why he'd been triggered to start using again. Yes, a crime had been committed. But this man was an Army veteran. He was in his mid-fifties. He had already demonstrated that he had the ability to change his life. Normally, in a case like that, you'd expect the court to put him in treatment rather than prison. But one day, after showing up for several court appearances, our client went missing. It was on a Friday; I was there in the courtroom, his lawyer was there—we were all there, except for this guy.

"I was so upset. On Saturdays I had my social work practice class, and I told the professor, 'All he had to do was show up! All he has to do is come to court!' And in a sweet, bemused way my professor said, 'No. He doesn't.'

"In retrospect, it's such a clear, simple thing. But at the time, it was a revelation. All of a sudden I felt like I was drifting in the middle of the ocean. I was on a different planet. That advice was so right, the way it helped me recognize the limits of my role. I was there to accompany people on whatever paths they had chosen to take—not just the ones that I deemed to be 'best' for them. It was a lesson about empathy, too. You can't support people if and only if they agree to do what you've told them to do. That's not an honest path. It doesn't work. If that's how you approach it, no one's going to believe you when you tell them you're there to help. Several times I've encountered people who have never been helped before by anybody. They've never met someone who cares. How can I step in, in that situation—how can I tell them, 'It's different now'—unless I'm willing to be there when they do something that doesn't seem to be in their best interests? What I realized that day was it isn't my job to save people. I recognized that I was going to fail and have to forgive myself for those failures."

What John had learned, although he may not have put

it this way at the time, was that he had to meet his clients where they were.

Social workers learn to ask themselves: *What does the* client *want? What are* their *goals? Are they ready and open for change?*

Pushing the client too hard tends to damage the client–social worker relationship. The client may become defensive and even more resistant to change. But by working collaboratively with clients, and helping them set their own goals, the social worker can guide them toward achieving the change that they want.

The veteran John had been assigned to help showed up in court the following week.

"I'd only known him to be kindly, soft-spoken," John says. "He liked to smile and was easy to get along with. But now he was angry. For him, it had been one court appearance too many. He said, 'I've done this before. I'm not going to jump through hoops for these people.' And because I had spoken to my professor, I was in a better position to understand him. Instead of becoming angry at him, I became angry *with* him. Now we were angry about the same thing, and that showed him that I had heard him. It showed him he wasn't alone. It strengthened our rapport and when I asked him to go into the courtroom and abide by his lawyer's suggestions—when I told him the outcome would be good if he did—he said that he would, and he did. That's something I might not have known how to do if my professor hadn't encouraged me to see the situation through my client's eyes and feel what he was feeling."

As HIS FIRST YEAR in social work school drew to a close, John landed a prestigious paid fellowship at the Memorial Sloan Kettering Cancer Center—ten weeks, starting in June, that were designed to prepare him for a difficult yearlong field placement at the hospital.

In hospital settings, social workers function as the patient hub, guiding clients through mind-numbing policies, procedures, and bureaucracies. They advocate for patients on concrete matters, like insurance and disability claims, and arrange discharge planning. A hospital social worker might provide emotional support to family members of patients who have just received terminal diagnoses or explain the details of such diagnoses to the patients themselves while offering resources and referrals. In a psychiatric setting, a social worker might run family meetings and group therapy, conduct one-on-one therapy sessions, and work collaboratively with patients to strengthen their support networks. In neonatal intensive care units, social workers might call child protective services (in cases of children born with positive toxicology reports) or assess new mothers for symptoms of postpartum depression. In an emergency room, social workers provide crisis counseling, help triage accident victims, diagnose and assess mental health patients, and manage end-of-life issues such as organ and tissue donations.

At Sloan Kettering, John was under the impression that he would be providing support for people with terminal conditions. But he didn't know exactly what he'd be doing until his first day at the hospital, when he was introduced to his supervisor and sent to work on the floor where leukemia patients were being treated. "Some of them were on death's door," he says. "Others were suffering from infections that prevented them from receiving chemotherapy. Some had been discharged and brought back again and again. Others had only just been diagnosed, and were lucky enough to have landed a spot at Sloan Kettering. One family had flown up from South America: the mother was ill, there were two adult children, and the father did not speak a word of English. The mother had an infection, and as a result, she wasn't being treated yet. Even so, they were being charged more than a hundred thousand dollars a month."

It was a level of stress and intensity beyond anything he had anticipated. As a medic, John had worked through enemy attacks and emergencies. But in Iraq and Afghanistan the moments of tension had been like fireworks going off in the middle of a long, hot afternoon. At Sloan Kettering they were endless and relentless, and he made his share of mistakes. One of the patients John saw was a woman who had survived breast cancer, gotten married, given birth, and then been diagnosed with leukemia. This woman understood that Sloan Kettering was a research hospital, a nonprofit where people from all walks of life were being treated. She knew that, in certain cases, funds were available to support and incentivize patients to keep up with experimental treatments. She herself was in financial distress, and as eager as he was to put her at ease, John ended up promising more than he could deliver.

"I knew about the money," he explains. "I didn't know exactly how the money worked, and told my patient that she could get financial assistance on the front end. It turned out that assistance was only available on the back end. When that became clear, I looked really bad. Here was this woman who'd survived cancer, gone on with her life. She had a young daughter now and, in all likelihood, she was not going to make it: her first cycle of treatment had had no effect, which is a bad sign, always. This mishap had made it impossible for me to continue to be her social worker, and that was bad, too, because she could have used a good social worker just then."

There were successes on the leukemia floor. "One small victory," John remembers, "was negotiating to get a Spanish translator to come to each morning's rounds so that the father from the South American family could pose his questions directly. That sounds like a small thing but it wasn't, because his kids would ask me in English, I'd ask the doctor, I'd get back to them, and I could see that a lot was getting lost in this game of telephone. I could see how agitated the father became. And I knew that the hospital had translators on staff, but it wasn't so easy to corral them because everyone was always so busy and the stakes were always so high. You had to insist."

John did insist. The father ended up getting answers in his own language, and for his family it made a tremendous difference. But it wasn't until a social worker downstairs on the thoracic floor went on vacation for several weeks that John found his place in the hospital and in his field.

On the leukemia floor, John was exposed to the widest variety of symptoms, conditions, and prognoses. Patients were constantly going on and off treatment; some were depressed or despondent and others were almost joyous. On the thoracic floor, the cases were likely all terminal. The air was more still. Some social workers in training would have found it to be too monotonous, too grim. But every time John filled in on that floor, he felt as though he was tapping a new set of skills, thoughts, and feelings.

Sooner or later social workers learn that coming into close proximity with death can be disorienting and dark, but it's also a gift and a privilege—hard but deeply human. John found that the connections he forged on the inside of that space were life-altering. "Something I was attuned to unconsciously evolved into an understanding and then a guiding principle," he explains. "When someone is staring death in the face, they want to turn their gaze elsewhere. And whatever it is they'll be looking at then is going to be the most important thing in their life. You have to figure out what that thing is, and sometimes it's the tiniest thing. In that environment the smallest answer to the smallest of questions can mean a great deal. Sometimes being present and knowing how to listen is all that it takes."

One of John's professors told him that people who are drawn to social work and other helping professions tend to have bad boundaries. For obvious reasons this can create problems. But in practice, John found the question of boundaries to be much more fluid, nuanced, and complicated. "Janet Malcolm's book on psychoanalysis is called *The Impossible Profession*," he says. "The same could be said of social work, but for different reasons. One thing I finally had to accept, in the face of incurable, unfixable suffering—whenever I felt helpless or overwhelmed—was that the most important factor I had to deal with wasn't pain, or the treatment, or even the outcome. Perhaps the most and the least I could do for a client when they were at their most vulnerable was just to let my compassion be felt. Social workers are uniquely trained and uniquely situated in their myriad professional placements to do this: to manage the precarious distance between individuals without being crushed and without further accentuating the necessary separation; to navigate impossible relationships and situations."

———

THOSE THREE WEEKS ON the thoracic floor set John on a path, but up on the leukemia floor—where happier outcomes were possible—he couldn't shake the feeling that he was failing his clients.

"We can fix this," John's supervisor told him. "You can do the work. You *are* doing the work."

Still, John had doubts, and in his seventh week of the ten-week fellowship, he dropped out. It was too late now to find another field placement. The decision meant that he'd have to spend an extra year in social work school, and John put that time to good use. He went into psychoanalysis, going three times a week. Those sessions helped him understand what it was like to be a patient. They yielded concrete results, too, he says, in terms of understanding his own motivations and drives, and directly informed the work he does now.

As an example, he mentions the Army.

"In analysis, I realized how much my personality and all the choices I'd made had been formed by competition within the household I grew up in: by my older brother, who was successful financially; by my father, who was a military man and also the son of a military man," John says.

"Going into the Army was a way to compete in the most concrete way with them both. Out of all of the dozens of reasons I might have made up in the month prior to enlisting and all the months I spent wondering, 'What am I doing here?' it had never occurred to me, until I went into therapy, that I was trying to win. That was incredibly important to me, because I'd been bowled over by several concepts I had learned in social work school. Ego psychology had been a pretty significant lesson, and cognitive distortions. But it's one thing to learn about modes of treatment like cognitive behavior therapy and another to recognize cognitive distortions within yourself. And once you understand what those distortions look like from the inside—once you see some of the ways in which we tend to misinterpret the world—you're in a much stronger position to spot it in others."

The work John was doing in analysis showed in the classroom. His fellow students recognized it. His professors did, too, and they started treating John more like a peer.

In October, John started to do volunteer work at the Hospice of New York. "I did what I should have done instead of going to Sloan Kettering," he says. "I started to work with people who were dying, rather than patients who were stuck on this merry-go-round of treatment and suffering."

As he visited clients in their homes, John took advantage of lessons he'd learned at Sloan Kettering. One patient was struggling to manage symptoms of dementia; John made a calendar with her to help make sense of the weeks and the days. Other patients—like a psychoanalyst who had made a hash of his own life—took more work. "Some would go over all the mistakes they had ever made. In ego psychology, that recounting is viewed as an attempt to create ego integrity: 'Did I lead a good life?' But the psychoanalyst had disappointed everyone who'd mattered to him: his children. His former wife. Now he was sick and dying and truly alone. But because I was a social work student and had been newly introduced to psychoanalysis myself, I could play the role of admiring him in the way he wanted to be admired. He was obsessed with Herodotus, the Greek historian, and with oracular visions in Herodotus, and he insisted that we collaborate on a book about all of the instances of premonitions that characters had had based on their dreams. Sitting with him, talking about that topic—I think it made him feel like his life hadn't been pointless."

By the time John interviewed with the Office of the Chief Medical Examiner, all of these experiences had cohered into a highly desirable package—for the job John ended up in, at least. But at first, in the interview, it wasn't entirely clear that the office knew what it was looking for. "There was a cop in the room," John recalls. "There was a detective, and an executive assistant district attorney, because the grant behind this program was coming out of the DA's budget. The first deputy chief medical examiner, who was a forensic pathologist, was there, along with an epidemiologist assigned to the medical examiner's office. There was a data analyst, too, and a liaison between the OCME and the Department of Health.

"They told me what I would be getting at the start of a case: files and photographs from the scene investigation; medical records; arrest records. All of this data but no through line, no narrative. And I had done nothing with my life but read novels and watch films. I had worked as a video editor. It made sense to me that what they were asking for was someone who could tell stories using these scattered bits of information. I don't know that they knew it, but I said, 'This is what you want me to do,' and they had an *aha* moment there in the room. There was my lived experience as well. I told them that I had lost people myself. I don't think they understood quite how closely, that I could have been one of these cases . . . But I was open about it. All in all, it just felt like my job: something I was destined to do. But even then I wasn't so sure that I wanted it."

A few days later, when the Office of the Chief Medical Examiner called with an offer, John was still of two minds. At first he didn't commit. Then an executive assistant district attorney called and left a long voice mail for John: "We're going to do such great work. You've been doing such great work. And together we're going to reduce overdoses. We're going to change the world. Everyone's going to be looking at us."

"I don't know who this guy was," John says, "but he must have been a Svengali or some sort of sorcerer. He was extremely convincing, and I drank the Kool-Aid and stayed in New York."

JOHN WORE A SUIT to his first day of work at the Office of the Chief Medical Examiner. One of the first conversations he had was with the first deputy chief medical examiner, the doctor who had attended John's job interview. He was now John's supervisor, and John asked him, "Do we provide bereavement services or bereavement referrals?"

The answer, in brief, was no. In the doctor's experience, social workers were people who did discharge planning rather than support. But thanks to John's work at Sloan Kettering and the subsequent work and volunteering he'd done, the bar for what he could accomplish was significantly higher than his employers had first thought. In his first hours on the job, John was starting to recognize deficits in services that he could hopefully start to address. And as the weeks passed and his supervisor, the first deputy chief medical examiner, began to see what social workers could accomplish, the supervisor became an extraordinary advocate and requested funds from the city for an entire social work department within the OCME. And at the same time, the rest of the ME's staff had gone from having no experience with social workers to valuing John more and more. One thing they discovered was that John could relieve them of the burden of providing causes of death over the phone. If families had medical questions John couldn't answer, he would email the ME who had conducted the autopsy and signed the death certificate— but that rarely happened. Within six months of arriving at the OCME, John was authorized to hire a second social worker. He had a colleague now—someone to process his experience with—and together they came to appreciate how much more they could do for the families.

Thus, competence—another core value of the National Association of Social Workers code of ethics—came into play.

Competence can be applied any number of ways, but in John's little corner at the OCME it involved learning that the best thing he could give people was answers. John couldn't always give families the answers they wanted, but more often than not—and this was a point of pride for John—the person on the phone ended the call by thanking him.

"Imagine that," John says. "I'm calling to ask them all these intrusive questions and I get a thank-you. Why? Because I know about drug users—I was one—and I can help them better understand. Because I'm staring at a case file and I know what happened; they don't have to go through the shame of telling me. Because I know how the OCME works and they can have my phone number. They want information. They want a better outcome or some measure of finality. They want understanding. If I know what they want, I can help them. This is competency by rote."

If a father or mother asked John if their son or daughter had suffered, he could answer with confidence, *No. Due to the analgesic and sedating properties of the drug your son [or daughter] was using, he [or she] had no awareness of what was happening. Long before the heart stops, the brain is no longer receiving oxygen, and neural activity stops. He [or she] felt no pain.*

John could sometimes estimate time of death to assure people there was nothing they could have done—that their loved one was already dead long before they called or knocked on their door. In this way death became less mysterious and more manageable.

Before long, John started offering a broader range of bereavement services. It wasn't exactly a part of his mandate, but it wasn't as if he had started to color outside of the lines.

One day he found himself speaking to Frank, the father of a thirty-two-year-old man who had died from a heroin overdose. Frank's son had died at home in the bathroom down the hall from his parents' bedroom, and Frank described the ten cops who'd come upstairs and barred him from seeing the body. His pain was incredibly raw, and John realized, in the course of their very first conversation, that he was going to have to do more than gather the data and cast it in narrative form.

Like his own father—and like his father's father before him and his three sons after him—Frank had grown up in Throggs Neck, in the Bronx. All in all, four generations of Italian Americans grew up in the same sprawling two-story house across the street from Saint Raymond's Cemetery. It was a house on the corner, on a lovely lot with a small pond, and the family was large and close-knit—old-world, in its way. It was as warm, safe, and secure as any background that John could imagine.

Frank told John about all three of the sons he had raised there. The oldest was an architect now, the youngest a research scientist. The middle son—the decedent—struggled with substances for most of his life: marijuana in high school, but that was just teenage stuff; Frank didn't think too much about it. By the time Frank's son turned seventeen, he was arrested for selling ecstasy. He started using cocaine and drinking heavily. Frank described a long history of rehab and relapse: his son's last two inpatient admissions had lasted for more than a year. At home the boy lied, stole to feed his addiction, fought with his parents. Once, while intoxicated, he assaulted Frank and Frank's father—an incident that led to ten weeks' confinement on Rikers Island. Two weeks after he was discharged, he went back to using.

Frank told John about an overdose his son had had eighteen months before his death. Frank and his wife had answered their doorbell and found him kneeling on the front step with his head against the front door. They called 911, and when the ambulance arrived paramedics administered Narcan (naloxone). Even then Frank hadn't understood that his son had started to use heroin.

After that Frank's son went into rehab. When he came out, he had prescriptions for risperidone, an antipsychotic shown to alleviate heroin cravings, and an antianxiety drug called Buspar (buspirone). He joined a gym and applied to train for a job as an electrician. One day he went out with Frank and Frank's father to shop for new clothes and sneakers. It was a wonderful day, Frank told John. His son had come into Frank's bedroom smiling. He told his parents that he felt good, that he loved them. That was the night Frank tried to open the bathroom door and could not because his son's body was jammed up against it.

As John worked to get all the details he'd gathered into his narrative there were a couple of things that stood out in sharp contrast: the five hundred friends who had come to the wake. The note of acceptance from a school for electricians, which had arrived in the mail one day after Frank's son's death. The apology note he had written his parents in rehab.

"I should be apologizing to *him*," Frank told John.

As a matter of course, John does not leave the office. In this case he did. Out in Throggs Neck he met with Frank and his family. He sat with them for a long time, across the street from the cemetery where Frank's son was now

Again and again, John found himself talking to families who needed more services than he could offer. And after two years on the job he was starting to feel that the other work he was doing was disappearing into a vacuum.

"I found myself thinking about the way my work was being used—about whether or not it was useful," he recalls. "At the same time, I was becoming aware that my understanding of the 'underlying causes' I had been looking for differed from what my employers were seeking. As a member of the medical examiner's office, I was working for the Department of Health. But the DA's office was paying my salary, out of a grant administered by the Office of National Drug Control Policy's High Intensity Drug Trafficking Areas [HIDTA] program. There were tensions built into that setup, because HIDTA wanted to find ways to use my rapport with family members to pursue a law enforcement agenda, while the DOH wanted to know about naloxone use and whether messaging efforts were making an impact. That was one side of the equation. And then I realized there was a disconnect between the things I had been looking for and the things I had been asked to discover."

———

AS A SOCIAL WORKER, John had been trained to look at social determinants of health. As a social worker assigned to the ME's office, he looked for the role those determinants played in substance use outcomes. But John now realized that things were more nuanced—more troubling—than anything the systems he was working inside of could process. Where did a person like Frank's son fit into the picture? What was the takeaway there? Certainly there were categories that people seemed to match. But when he looked at his cases in aggregate, John saw more and more exceptions, outliers, and unaccountable breaks in the expected patterns.

What's the relationship, he asked himself, *between an overworked emergency room nurse who dies from a Valium overdose while sleeping off her shift and a teenage fentanyl user found on the floor of a Starbucks bathroom on the Upper West Side? Nothing? Everything?*

In a way, John was wrestling with contradictions he himself had created: to pluck out the details that make up a life, and turn those details into a compelling story, is to highlight all the ways in which that one life is unique. This was something John was especially well equipped to do. As a former video editor and a voracious reader, he understood narratives. As a social worker, he'd been trained to see every client as an individual—to "meet them where they were"— and tailor his services to their specific needs. But that wasn't what the system was asking for now. The system was asking John for commonalities.

Then again, the position John found himself in also cut straight to a problem with social work as a whole: the plain fact that people are people and systems are systems; social workers may well be the grease in the gears, but every once in a while someone's going to get crushed.

That's why self-care is so vital when it comes to social work: basic things, like exercise, diet, and downtime. Ideally, social workers have supervisors who pay close attention and notice symptoms of secondary traumatic stress. But it's also equally important to keep the big picture in mind. If the system worked perfectly well, it wouldn't need you. But that alone doesn't make you the right fit for the system you're in. Sometimes the job is impossible. Sometimes it's just not for you. Either way, knowing when to walk can be crucial.

For John, a number of factors came into play.

Those meetings at One Police Plaza, for instance. At first John had found them inspiring. It was deeply validating for him and his colleagues to hear his narratives read out loud to a roomful of civic leaders. But as the months passed John grew disillusioned. He recalls one case involving a woman who had been raped by a family friend when she was a teenager. He also recalls that the executive assistant DA—the same "Svengali" who had talked John into the job—instructed him to leave that rape out when paring the narrative down for the meeting. "Adverse childhood event" was the phrase John had to use instead of "sexual assault," and that piece of information got distilled into an epidemiological report where "ACE Trauma" was classified as one category among several and assigned no more weight than any of the others.

"It didn't matter that a woman had been raped, that a young man had lost his mother," John says. "It didn't matter what had happened to them, the specific circumstance. It was: 'Childhood trauma is a risk factor. Check.'"

From the executive assistant DA's perspective, useful information looked more like: "The decedent's mother said he had been buying drugs online." Useful, because it was measurable and actionable: if enough overdose victims bought drugs online, more resources could be allocated to trying to shut down online drug markets. But what could the DA's office do with something that had happened five years ago— or fifty?

From John's perspective, the specific circumstances mattered a great deal. Perhaps the woman who had been raped by a family friend had been told not to talk about it. Now she had a secret. John knew, when a person has one secret, it's easier to have many secrets. And in John's experience, secrets could kill.

More and more, John felt, those meetings were becoming performances, ways for city officials to enact and celebrate their civic virtue without having to make the difficult calls. As time went on, officials from other cities began to show up at the meetings. Coincidentally or not, city officials who were likely to be asked questions at the meetings now seemed to be getting those questions in advance. And as the meetings grew more peformative, the chances that meaningful change would come out of them seemed to grow slimmer. At the same time, John noticed, the meetings decreased in frequency from once every three months to once every four.

When John accepted the job, he'd bought into the notion that the OCME could transform itself, at the atomic level, from an organization that only investigated deaths into an organization that also tried to prevent them. To imagine that a city agency could do this sounds naïve—almost remarkably so. But was it? Thanks in large part to John's efforts, his supervisor, the first deputy chief medical examiner, had bought into the notion as well. He, too, had seen that there was a large piece missing in terms of what the OCME could do. Among other things, John's supervisor wanted to have social workers on staff 24-7 in all five boroughs. That way, if a medicolegal investigator arrived on a scene and found the deceased person they'd been called out for surrounded by other people who were high, the MLI could call for someone to assist and possibly save the lives of the living.

John's supervisor also wanted to expand the program John was a part of to include *all* death investigations. If you know someone who died of a drug overdose, there's a far greater chance that you'll die of an overdose, too. If you know someone who got shot, the chances that you'll get shot as well are also exponentially higher. After seeing what John could do the first deputy chief medical examiner wanted to expand social determinant investigations to include everybody.

That wasn't the OCME's mandate. But the first deputy chief medical examiner was a doctor as well as an administrator. It was hard to stand by when so many were suffering and so many were dying. He was willing to change the department. But his department was one of many within a Department of Health that was, in turn, one of many departments inside a giant web of city agencies. For now, there was no funding. But John's supervisor was a lifer at the Office of the Chief Medical Examiner. No matter what, he would keep plugging away.

In that sense, John hadn't been naïve at all. He had dared to dream that things could be different. Without that impulse—which is central to social work—no change at all would be possible.

At the same time, John felt that he'd done all he could for the office. The point was driven home every time he finished one of his narratives and uploaded it into the OCME's case management system. Forget those meetings at One Police Plaza: this was his job at the most basic level. If he couldn't get the city to put his data to good use, perhaps future researchers could. But there was a problem here, too: the case management system had been designed to process any number of forms. It collected and collated data but it didn't know what to do with a narrative, and all the ones John uploaded went into the system as scans—which made them all but impossible to search and collate. Whether or not anyone would take the time to read through them was anyone's guess. And so, as John's second year at the medical examiner's office drew to a close, he made peace with the fact that, for him, it was time to stop guessing. In 2020, just before COVID-19 deaths in New York City started to spike, he resigned.

COVID-19 overwhelmed the Office of the Chief Medical Examiner just as it overwhelmed the city's hospitals and morgues. On any given day in the past, John's colleagues would have been opening twenty-five to forty investigations into sudden unexplained deaths. Now those numbers shot up by a factor of ten and then doubled again. The social worker John had brought on board was reassigned to process suspected COVID-19 fatalities—something she did to the exclusion of everything else for the rest of the spring and well into the summer—and when she and John spoke now, it was over the phone, because John had gone back to the desert, where he'd felt at home ever since his time in New Mexico.

Cynically, one could say that all the narratives John worked to assemble were now lying unread in the medical examiner's computers, like so many unvisited graves. But for John there was still cause for hope, because, even though they they had devolved into political theater, those meetings had had an effect. Other jurisdictions *had* taken notice. There was another pilot program now, in Philadelphia— one that involved anthropologists as well as social workers. And in Ocean County, New Jersey, social workers had started to investigate six overdoses a month—a high number for a place that sees far fewer deaths than New York City—and holding meetings monthly to address the crisis. The irony was not lost on John: Ocean County was now utilizing the kind of information he'd learned to gather in ways that New York, with all its wealth and its resources, was not. But social change doesn't take place overnight, and out in the desert John's sense of irony was tempered by hope —and by pride in the work that he had done.

3

WENDY DOUCETTE

When people think of social workers, they often imagine dowdy, disheveled crusaders—mostly women—with sensible shoes, crazy hair, and bleeding hearts. Wendy Doucette, a social worker who is a psychotherapist in private practice, does not wear clogs. She does not stick a pencil in her hair to keep her bun up. She's passionate about the work that she does, but there's nothing disheveled about her. Wendy is warm and outgoing, with long auburn hair that hangs in loose curls. She favors a natural look but isn't afraid of lipstick. There's a psychiatrist in Los Angeles who looked at her once and said, "You're a social worker? Where's your beaded necklace and hippie skirt?" Wendy didn't take it as an insult; she laughed instead and developed a strong professional relationship with the psychiatrist. She receives referrals from him to this day. As a therapist, and as a woman who runs her own business, Wendy looks to make connections.

It helps that Wendy is genuinely interested in the people who cross her path. She chats with her barista at Starbucks and with the woman who makes the sandwiches she eats for lunch. She makes small talk in the elevator up to her office and is on a first-name basis with the dry cleaners in her neighborhood. In New York, one of her best friends once told her, "If you keep talking to the bus drivers, everyone will think you're a tourist." Somehow, no one ever did. Wendy is quick to smile and pull people in. She's disarming and, above all, curious. People—all people—are a puzzle that she wants to solve. In the course of a day, she may try to figure out when a friend's husband became so withdrawn, why an old client started drinking again, or how the young woman who's started to beg on her corner came to be homeless and what the best way to help her find a place to sleep might be. These puzzles give Wendy a sense of purpose. They keep her intellectually engaged and emotionally involved, even as they pay her bills. Personally and professionally, she thinks of herself as incredibly fortunate.

Wendy knows social workers who took a straight shot to private practice—who went to social work school, completed two years of field placement, and took their first jobs at clinics with an eye toward hanging their own shingles out as quickly as possible. Wendy never had such a linear focus. She started on her path to the profession in high school, when her grandfather died of leukemia. At home, no one had ever talked about his illness. It wasn't until he'd gone into the hospital that Wendy understood how sick he'd become. The hospital's staff and its social workers made a deep impression on her. They were gentle but also direct and honest. In retrospect, it would occur to her that empathy, honesty, and directness were qualities she possessed herself.

After her grandfather's death, Wendy attended Barnard College, graduating with a bachelor's degree in sociology. Although she had always loved psychology and thought that it would be her major, a sociology course called Deviance and Social Control set her on a different track. It showed Wendy that something was missing from psychology: the social aspect. She not only learned to consider a person in their environment but also became aware of the ways in which social policy shapes that environment. For Wendy, social work represented the marriage of these two ideas: studying individuals (their brains and behavior) as well as the social factors that shape them. This eventually led to a career as a therapist.

Many people who go to therapy assume they've been

referred to a psychologist. But very often the therapist is a social worker like Wendy, who has earned her clinical license. Day in and day out she sits in a room with her clients and listens. She guides. She highlights. She asks pointed questions, all the while keeping the bigger picture in mind: her clients' body language; their behaviors, their defenses, their sense of humor, their childhoods, their histories of trauma, and, most importantly, the things they want to change and how they can start to feel better.

CALIFORNIA SUNSHINE STREAMED INTO Wendy's office. She took note of Allison's clasped hands, the stiff way she sat at the edge of her chair, legs crossed underneath at the ankles. Allison's eyes shot up to the ceiling, then toward the door. She had come to the session in workout clothes. Dressed to run, she wouldn't have looked out of place if she bolted out of Wendy's office and kept going, straight up Santa Monica Boulevard.

Allison was the first client Wendy was meeting today. Just before she had come into the office, Wendy turned off the overhead light. Allison had once mentioned that she preferred natural light, and Wendy always tried to accommodate her. She opened the blinds as far as they'd go, and now she followed Allison's gaze as she looked out the window at the big tree outside.

That tree was the reason that Wendy had rented this office. Like all therapists, she tried to create an inviting environment. When someone walks into a warm, well-appointed office in a nice part of town, the $225 that they're going to be paying for a forty-five-minute session seems much more reasonable. But it was the tree that made this office special: the way its thick limbs and branches filled the window, casting warm shadows on the walls.

Wendy focused on Allison's breathing as well as her own. She had noticed years earlier that her New York speech patterns could strike Californians as a little too fast, a little too loud, a little too much. In the past they might have been too much for Allison. And so, as Wendy redirected Allison's gaze back from the tree into the room, she made an effort to speak more softly. Sitting back in her chair, she felt her body relax. She was modeling calm, and as she regulated herself, Wendy felt Allison beginning to co-regulate with her.

"I can't be home anymore," Allison said. "When I'm home, there's a stack of bricks on my chest. It's like there's a big, monstrous thing over there and it's going to swallow me."

Allison tended to speak in abstractions and Wendy often asked her to zero in: "Can you describe that monstrous thing in more detail?" But Allison was witty and self-aware, too. "I'm just like Cinderella," she had told Wendy the first time they'd met. "But the part where she was stuck with the evil stepmother. Not the part where the prince comes to save her. I'm still waiting for him."

Wendy recalled Allison's description of herself as an eight-year-old wearing long-sleeve shirts in summer to cover up bruises and burns. The burns had come from her stepmother's curling iron, the bruises from the brass buckle of her late father's leather belt. Allison's father had died when she was seven. After that, her stepmother started locking her in her room. She was allowed to use only one of the three bathrooms in the house. She was never, ever allowed to eat between meals. Allison's stepmother kept the refrigerator and all of the cabinets locked. She told Allison that she was needy and ugly and useless and fat. Once, the stepmother went on a shopping trip to the mall. Allison begged go with her. Rather than take her along, the stepmother locked Allison up in her room yet again. The child sat there alone for four hours trying not to pee.

Just before her stepmother came home, Allison did pee.

"Pull that crap again," her stepmother said, "and I'll send you to foster care."

Wendy understands the way abuse or neglect and trauma affects a child's developing brain—the way neural pathways form or fail to form. Trauma, in the form of neglect or abuse, can cause lasting changes in the areas of the brain that deal with stress: the amygdala, the hippocampus, and the prefrontal cortex. Extreme neglect and/or abuse can impair memory, learning, and behavior, and can actually shrink the size of the brain. Children who live in a constant state of stress do not learn how to regulate their emotions and have an increased risk of chronic disease and mental illness in adulthood. But neuroplasticity studies show that the brain continues to be malleable. "The good news," Wendy says, "is research has proven we can literally rewire our brains by way of secure attachments, effective interventions, and psychological treatment."

Wendy knew that the abuse Allison had suffered had thrust her into a permanent state of hypervigilance. She had nightmares. Certain sounds, sights, and smells brought back feelings of fear, although she could never identify the specific memories associated with those feelings. At her job, her need to please had served her well: she'd become highly successful in her field. In her interpersonal relationships it often caused problems. But for all that, Wendy understood Allison's resourcefulness and resilience.

As a child, Allison had learned to disappear. She'd become best friends with Holly, a girl who lived with her younger brother and two parents. Holly's mother was a stay-at-home mom. Holly's father was a lawyer in town. When things got especially bad at home, Allison spent days on end with Holly's family. She ate dinner there, ran family errands, helped in the garden, and went to the movies. She cleared plates, took out the garbage, said "Please" and "Thank you." In the mornings she woke up early, rolled up her sleeping bag, and tucked it away in the corner so that Holly's family would forget she had been there for even one night.

"You were so smart, so savvy at that age, to know what real safety looked like," Wendy told her. "What an *incredibly* resilient kid."

Allison didn't know how jarring it could be for Wendy to take it all in. It wasn't the evil stepmother stories that threw her; it was the disconnect between the highly functional adult Allison had become and the brutalized girl she kept locked up inside. Wendy could see that if *she* had trouble integrating the two Allisons, then Allison wouldn't be able to, either. She also saw how exhausting it was to be in a constant hypervigilant state.

Years earlier, Wendy had worked as a primary therapist and clinical supervisor at an in-patient addiction treatment facility in Malibu. There, she had been flooded with clients' traumas. There was always a moment, just after her clients detoxed, when they were at their most vulnerable. Buried memories came to surface. Some patients realized for the first time that they had been self-medicating in order to manage their mental illness.

"Initially, I was overwhelmed by the amount of trauma I was being exposed to," Wendy recalls. "Every kind of trauma: incest, rape, homelessness, gun violence. Complex trauma as well: 'My father started sexually abusing me when I was five and abandoned the family when I was fourteen.' It was a lot to take in."

This was pain that Wendy's clients carried inside of their bodies. It was embedded in their muscles and bones and coursed through their nervous systems. Like Allison today, they had found themselves in a safe space, but their brains and their bodies hadn't caught up. They had been stuck in a state of hypervigilance, too.

"I don't know why I'm anxious all the time," Allison said.

"I'm especially anxious when I'm alone. That's when it's the hardest. Why can't I just relax?"

Wendy could have told her, then and there, in technical terms. She could have explained the way Allison's brain had developed or described her attachment disorders. But a therapist can't just break clients open, have them relive the worst parts of their childhoods, diagnose them, and send them out into the world. "Some people have the idea that bringing trauma back up in the room is essential," Wendy says. "Actually, it can be heavy and brutal and counterproductive. You don't want and don't need to have your clients reliving their childhoods all the time, even—especially—when that's where the trauma resides. Early in my career, I worked with a client whose gym teacher had sexually abused her when she was a teen. I listened quietly as she recalled keeping all the lights off in her house and hiding on the dirt floor of her basement while the teacher waited outside in his car, looking for her. By the time her forty-five minutes were up, my client was sobbing. I got her upright and out the door but I spent the rest of the night worried about her. Today, I wouldn't follow a client's lead like that. If they're reliving the past and reliving their trauma, that means they're getting activated again. They're no longer with *you*. They're back there, with the trauma. It's the opposite of the reaction you want."

"Here's the thing," Wendy told Allison. "Fundamentally, kids need to feel safe. And you didn't."

"I was *never* safe," Allison said.

"Can you remember a time when, maybe, you did feel safe?"

"Curling up in my grandmother's lap, before she died. When it was just the two of us and I could be near her quietly. It was very comforting. I just liked being near her."

"That sounds so nice."

Wendy was using her soft voice again. She smiled. She leaned forward.

"Do me a favor," she said. "Take that in. When you were little and you could just sit with your grandmother. When you didn't need to talk and you could just kind of hang out. Take it in. See if you can go there in your mind. Close your eyes if you want. You don't have to."

Allison did close her eyes. For Wendy, that was an encouraging sign. She stopped talking too, sat with the moment, and honored it. When Wendy's clients went deep and quiet like this, it was a sure sign that therapy was working—that they were letting her in and allowing her to help them.

That they trusted her. Part of Wendy's job was to spot these windows of opportunity and make the best of them.

Allison sank back into her chair.

"It's different, right?" Wendy said. "What you're feeling? What do you notice inside?"

"I'm calmer."

"Yes. You did that on your own. You showed your brain something that felt safe. You showed yourself something that felt a lot calmer. That's *all* you did, but how amazing is it that you were able to shift your entire nervous system and slow yourself down just by thinking?"

Allison opened her eyes and looked straight at Wendy— not at the ceiling, out the window, or into her lap.

"This is what happens with trauma: the good and the bad," Wendy continued. "Your mind is remembering this stuff all the time. Your body is responding to the fear by staying on high alert. It makes total sense, given the way you grew up."

"Okay," Allison said.

"But being on high alert all the time doesn't make much sense now. It no longer fits in with your life. And you being calmer today—you feeling safe, whether or not you're alone—is the kind of stuff that we can work on in here. You'll be surprised at how much we'll accomplish."

"Do you really think so?"

"Yes," Wendy said. "I really do."

HERE'S SOMETHING WENDY NOTICED early on in her training: if you ask a social worker what they learned in the classroom, they're bound to say, "I don't remember." But ask a social worker what they learned in their two years interning in the field, and inevitably they will say, "Everything." Even if the first year's a disaster, students tend to wise up. There's not much hand-holding in a field placement. If anything, the graduate school system takes the opposite tack. Schools want their students to navigate and tolerate broken systems, manage without supervision, and work with limited resources. Seasoned social workers tend to tell students to keep their fears to themselves. If the placement office at your school knows that you're wary of working with victims of domestic violence, your first year will be spent in a women's shelter. If you find kids boring, you'll end up interning at an elementary school. A more experienced social worker might say, "Keep your mouth shut and hope for the best."

Social work school isn't really about school at all. It's

about getting thrown into the ocean and proving that you can not only swim but also make it to shore.

For Wendy's first year of field placement, New York University sent her to intern at Federation Employment and Guidance Service (FEGS). FEGS, which was founded in 1934, was once one of the largest nonprofits in New York City. At its peak the organization served almost 2 million people, providing education, career development, behavioral health, family services, home care, and rehabilitation, as well as support for people with developmental disabilities. And in 1996—a decade before the agency filed for bankruptcy, abruptly, and shuttered its doors, shocking the nonprofit world—Wendy was a twenty-five-year-old intern in a FEGS day treatment program in Manhattan.

Three days out of the week she worked with clients who had diagnoses of schizophrenia, personality disorders, schizoaffective disorder, and bipolar disorder. FEGS served a large population of clients who were deaf or hearing impaired; a large population of clients who were homeless, living in shelters, or living in supportive housing; and a large population of clients with intellectual disabilities. Wendy recalls walking into the office, looking around, and thinking, *What the fuck is this and how the fuck am I going to do it?*

Above all, she was afraid that, because she had no idea what she was doing, she wouldn't be able to make a difference in clients' lives. These clients had had their challenges, but they'd been around the block, too. They knew much more than Wendy did about poverty and neglect. They were also used to getting passed off to a new, inexperienced social work intern every time September rolled around. When Wendy sat down with her first client—a forty-year-old woman who regularly got into physical altercations at her homeless shelter—Wendy suggested that they work on managing the woman's anger.

"Amy was my therapist last week and now suddenly you're my therapist?" the client said, rolling her eyes. "You don't even know me. You think you can tell me what to do?"

"You're right, I don't. Why don't you tell me what you want to work on?"

"I got the CIA bugging my room. Why don't we work on that?"

Wendy was in deep water. But as she worked, she learned more than she ever had studying the manual of mental disorders for class. She also started to understand that many of the diagnoses and medications she'd been interested in in the abstract could amount to life sentences out in the world.

Each diagnosis was a box—clients were grouped together in boxes—and this was, ultimately, dehumanizing. If she knew that a client was schizophrenic before meeting him, Wendy could feel her own inherent bias. She was young, but she was eager and learning quickly. She wanted to know everything. Unfortunately, the supervisor she'd been assigned to didn't go out of her way to answer any of Wendy's questions.

"I didn't know what I was doing," Wendy says. "What I needed, or what I *thought* I needed, was hand-holding and guidance. My supervisor was more like 'Figure it out on your own.' She didn't coddle, or hand-hold, or nurture. It wasn't even that she was a bad supervisor. It was just a bad fit, given what I needed at the time. Working with chronically mentally ill clients was overwhelming. If she had said, 'This is how you build rapport . . . This is how you make a treatment plan,' I may not have relied so heavily on my instincts. Today I rely heavily on my instincts. Back then I was just starting out. But then again, it's social work: there's no one right way to do it. The concrete stuff, like documenting your cases, can be taught in the classroom. But how to treat someone with schizophrenia? There's no one way to do that. As it was, I was forced to figure it out on my own and find ways to connect with my clients outside of talk therapy, which is what I initially thought I would be doing. I learned on my own that when someone is chronically paranoid, you don't tell them whatever they think isn't true. I learned what it's like to just sit still with someone who's psychotic."

Forced to rely on herself, Wendy made a conscious effort to shake off her fear and at least feign confidence. *This is what I want to be: a social worker,* she said to herself. *In order to be a good one, I need to be flexible. I need to meet my clients where they are and support them as they set their own goals. I need to dig in, dive in, and learn enough about my clients to connect with them.* But while she helped clients meet the goals they had set for themselves—even those that involved CIA operations—Wendy also worked on her own concrete goals: getting her clients to take medication, helping them apply for benefits, securing housing for them.

Questions that would have bewildered her earlier turned out to have answers: "How do I run three groups a day, with fifteen or twenty psychotic clients, when all hell keeps breaking loose in the room?"

The solution that Wendy came up with for that one was simple: arts and crafts.

———

AFTER HER FIRST YEAR of field placement, Wendy attended a New York University seminar on social work and spirituality. One of the lectures she heard there, by an art therapist who worked with terminally ill children, struck a chord. That night Wendy found herself thinking of her grandfather. She understood that her mother's decision to keep his leukemia diagnosis a secret stemmed from a protective impulse. But that NYU seminar helped her see that people can talk about difficult things in ways her own family never could. For several years now she had wished she had known about her grandfather's illness before he'd gone into the hospital. She would have spent so much more time with him. It was too late for that now, but the art therapist's lecture had opened a window into ways she could help other families cope.

The next day Wendy went straight to NYU's field placement office.

"I don't know if you'll let me do this, but I've just had an epiphany," she said. "I know exactly what I want to do. I want to work with kids who are dying. Can I do that for my second year placement?"

Most of the students in Wendy's program—particularly students who intended to build their own practices—were vying to secure field placements at psychoanalytic institutes. But for her second year of training, Wendy was assigned to the pediatric HIV department at Beth Israel hospital. Some of her clients were minimally impacted by their diagnosis. Others were living out their final days. Wendy served on an interdisciplinary team in tandem with doctors, psychiatrists, other therapists, and social workers, working with children from a wide range of socioeconomic backgrounds. As the year progressed, Wendy felt more and more confident on her morning rounds, where she presented her cases. She paid close attention to her more experienced colleagues, and this time around she loved her supervisor, a straight-talking woman who challenged Wendy at every turn.

"She pushed me to look at myself, my own losses and grief, and how those things were impacting the way I was working with these kids and their families," Wendy says. "In that way she was a bit like a therapist, asking me to look at my own history and my own background and showing me things I still needed to look at and heal."

Wendy recalls one case involving a dying child. "I didn't want to keep him alive, exactly," she says, "but I got overly invested and felt overly connected to him. There were times he didn't want to see me or talk—he was only nine!—but I felt very helpless and very up against the limitations of my role with him. My supervisor said, 'Do you want to make sure he stays alive another week? How are *you* going to do that? You want to make sure everything's peaceful and perfect and all the stars are aligned before he dies? Is that about him? Or is that about *you*?' I can still see her shaking her head as she says it. She didn't go in for 'This is so sad; he's so young.' She was not warm and fuzzy at all. But I learned more from her than from anyone else. When my expectations weren't realistic, she would point it out. She never shamed me but she did help me see what my biases were, how narrow my vision could be. Checking my own ego and preconceived ideas were things that I took from her."

By the time Wendy had finished her placement and graduate school she had all of the skills and all of the confidence that she needed for her first social work job, at the Payne Whitney psychiatric clinic on Manhattan's Upper East Side.

As a social worker assigned to the hospital's in-patient geriatric psychiatric unit, Wendy worked with elderly patients suffering from depression, delirium, and dementia. She ran groups, provided psychoeducation to family members, saw patients for individual sessions, and helped with insurance and discharge planning. The luckiest patients had good health insurance, support from family and friends, and secure housing. They were already in treatment with a psychiatrist and a therapist outside of the hospital. The less fortunate had lousy insurance or no insurance at all, no housing, and no mental health services. Wendy's job involved developing as much support for those clients as she could before they were discharged—even as their insurance companies pressed for the earliest possible discharge. It wasn't an easy balance to strike and Wendy spent a large part of each day battling insurance companies and signing patients up for Medicaid.

"I was burning out," Wendy recalls. "It was draining and stressful. The system was terribly flawed and it was so hard to do the things you thought were best for your clients."

Time and again Wendy noticed that the most compassionate, patient-centered insurance reviewers came from the Service Employees International Union, Local 32BJ, which represented the city's doormen, office cleaners, bus drivers, and maintenance workers. Reviewers from 32BJ always let patients stay until they had recovered fully. Wendy developed strong relationships with them and a year into her job at Payne Whitney she allowed herself to be recruited by the union. 32BJ offered her more money, a nicer office, and shorter work hours. But after a year with the union, Wendy started to wonder if she wasn't burning out on New York as well.

Several of Wendy's friends lived in Los Angeles. Her brother lived in West Hollywood. Wendy was still in her twenties and single. She didn't have kids. If she was going to jump, the timing would have to be right, and when the right job came along—at the AIDS Healthcare Foundation—the timing was perfect.

For two years Wendy provided counseling, ran groups, and participated in training at foundation clinics all over Los Angeles. Then, in 2002, she went to work in the home hospice care program at Cedars-Sinai Medical Center. This was a job with much more flexibility than Wendy had ever had. On most days, she carried a pager and went on home visits. She had to keep track of her hours, but Wendy could make her own schedule and she answered, mostly, to herself. If she started seeing private clients of her own, in the evenings, Wendy thought, it wouldn't impact her day job. Cedars-Sinai was paying her well. She had excellent health insurance. Wendy had worked and trained for eight years, earned her clinical hours in New York and California, and passed a rigorous oral exam that California administered for licensing at the time. (The oral exam was abolished shortly after Wendy took it, in 2002.) At thirty-two, Wendy was a fully licensed clinical social worker, perfectly positioned to start her own practice.

What that meant in practical terms was renting an office and sending an email blast out to her contacts, letting them know she was open for business.

One by one, Wendy hoped, the referrals would start to roll in.

HERE ARE SOME PRACTICAL tips on starting your own practice:

- Put a profile up in *Psychology Today* and purchase an advertisement.

- Reach out to anyone and everyone you know. Don't be shy about letting them know you're open for business.

- Work collaboratively with as many therapists, psychiatrists, and medical doctors as you can, and be sure to maintain those contacts. If they like you, they'll send you referrals.

- Build a warm, inviting website that also screams: *If you're looking at me, I have the expertise to make you feel better.*

- As soon as you're able to, specialize and narrow your professional focus. New therapists may take on all clients because they need as many clients as possible to stay afloat. But over time they'll hone in on the clients they can treat most effectively and with the most confidence. (Wendy refers to herself as a trauma therapist. Other therapists might specialize in adoption or addiction. There are children's therapists, couples therapists, divorce therapists, sex therapists . . . The list isn't endless, but it's not as short as you might think.)

- Learn the branding game. Wendy herself is old-school and relies on word-of-mouth, but some therapists hire branding consultants, develop short "elevator pitches," set up social media accounts, and launch blogs. In short, they do what they can to strategically market themselves.

Ideally, new therapists will attend every event they can get to. They will stay up-to-date on terminology and ever-evolving treatment modalities. Because it is reckless as well as exhausting to practice in a vacuum, they will set up individual or group supervision.

And there's one more trick to starting your new practice: You don't have to tell your first client that he or she is the one and only client you have.

That's the advice Wendy gave herself when she rented her first part-time office in 2003.

Most new therapists rent offices by the hour. Typically those offices are in anonymous buildings with anonymous rooms: a point person oversees all of the schedules and keeps track of the room assignments. The spaces are lousy, with knockoff furniture, pleather, and a Post-it on the door that reads, "In Session." Wendy wanted more than a Post-it. She didn't mind sharing a space but the thought of switching rooms all the time bothered her. The room she eventually found, in Santa Monica, was tiny, with a small couch and a kid-sized desk pressed up against the wall, but it was an office Wendy could return to. She rented it out for two nights a week before landing a single client.

Now that she had her own business and her own space, Wendy had to think about liability insurance and billing, record keeping, and taxes. But above all, she had to get clients.

Her first, a man in his twenties, was referred to her by a psychiatrist from the AIDS clinic. This client had long since come out as gay to his friends in Los Angeles but not to his family in Idaho. Although he was riddled with anxiety, he was mature enough to seek out the help he needed—and, just as Wendy had hoped, he had no idea that he was Wendy's first and only client.

Two weeks later she started seeing a middle-aged man who had never been able to sustain a romantic relationship. Two weeks after that, a thirty-eight-year-old woman walked into Wendy's office. She had been struggling with grief and loss after multiple miscarriages and several rounds of in vitro fertilization.

Private practice gave Wendy the flexibility to work part-time after she got married and had her own children; it was a great help after 2006, when Cedars-Sinai closed its home hospice program. But in 2011 Wendy and her husband split up and she realized that the practice alone would not keep her afloat. "I loved having my own business," she recalls, "but I needed much more security and felt that I needed to be around other people as well."

Wendy quickly found full-time work at an in-patient addiction treatment facility in Malibu and continued seeing clients in the evenings when her ex-husband had their children. She welcomed the challenge of going back to work full-time at the addiction treatment facility. It turned out to be a gift, watching clients who might have died get sober, seeing them get better, have relationships, land jobs, and have babies. But the flip side of that was seeing people overdose or commit suicide. In addiction it was one or the other—there wasn't much middle ground—and as a result, the job was always intense.

It's not unusual for young social workers to struggle with boundary issues. That's one of the reasons that good supervision is crucial: without it, it's easy to lose perspective. But in many cases supervisors themselves may be overwhelmed or distracted, distant, or otherwise unavailable, and in those cases social workers must remind themselves to stay within prescribed limits: to stop themselves from texting with clients; to avoid speaking with clients on their own off-hours; to refrain from speaking too freely about their own lives and desires. Even older social workers may find that some of these boundaries are easier to define than they are to enforce—because, by definition, social workers are dedicated to helping and effecting change in the lives of their clients. They've trained for years and dedicated their lives to a job that is rooted in empathy, and empathy demands a certain amount of identification. But too much identification can be a dangerous thing, and while Wendy kept most boundaries intact, she did find herself giving her cell phone number out to clients. She found herself cursing more, too, laughing more; invariably she would come home exhausted. Clients who were detoxing from drugs and alcohol were more emotionally open and more vulnerable than many of the clients she was seeing in her private practice. Professionally, this was exciting. Personally, it became harder to shut the job off at the end of the day.

Four years into the job, Wendy wasn't burning out, but she was starting to fray, and there were other downsides to working at the treatment facility. Sometimes staff members were laid off unceremoniously. Sometimes clients who'd been brought in on a sliding scale were simply dumped. This wasn't right, Wendy felt. These things didn't signal a healthy organization. And on top of all that, Wendy discovered that male colleagues who had less experience, less training, and fewer degrees than she did were earning more than she was making.

"I regret now that I didn't negotiate my salary," Wendy admits. "I was grateful to have a good job, grateful to have a good salary. But I should have asked for more money. Women are not trained or encouraged to negotiate. Men are. Add that to the fact that we didn't go into social work to make tons of money, which leads to our thinking, 'Oh, well, we'll take what we get.' And that's problematic as well."

Wendy did not want to abandon her clients. But as she wrestled with whether or not she should stay in the job, she became more and more certain that she did not want to work anywhere if she wasn't the one making the rules and dictating her own salary.

Finally, Wendy quit and went into private practice full-time.

"I liked the idea of being in control," she says. "I knew that the work could be isolating, but not having to ask for a vacation—that's a game changer. There's the flip side, of course, of not having paid vacations, or health insurance, but that's a trade-off that makes me want to hustle all the harder. For all the financial anxiety and the worry, I ended up making a nice living."

Wendy spent the next four years building her practice,

establishing her reputation, gathering word-of-mouth referrals, and attending trainings. Together with three therapists from different parts of the country (Portland, New York, and Chicago), all of whom she met during those trainings, she formed a group for peer supervision. She also countered the isolation of private practice by scheduling regular coffee, lunch, and drink dates with colleagues. Gradually, Wendy expanded her practice to include home visits with new mothers to provide postpartum emotional support. She expanded her outreach, attending networking events through the Beverly Hills Chamber of Commerce and perfecting her own elevator pitch: "I'm a psychotherapist, and what I love most is helping my clients get their minds updated so that past traumas no longer impair their ability to lead happy and healthy lives."

With each passing year, Wendy felt more empowered. She was running a practice on her own terms. She was more and more confident in her decision not to work for anyone else. She came to see herself as prospering, successful, and effective. At the same time, she made sure to leave several spots open for sliding-scale clients who couldn't pay her full fee. After all, Wendy may have been a psychotherapist, but she was also a social worker.

In other words, Wendy was just where she'd hoped she would be when she decided to practice full-time: in a room with a full slate of clients she knew she could help. Then, suddenly, with the arrival of COVID-19, she found herself in that same room alone.

Wendy pivoted quickly, transitioning to telemedicine right after Los Angeles went into lockdown. Most of her clients transitioned with her. At first she wasn't sure video sessions would work—so much of Wendy's job involved evaluating her clients' eye contact, their breathing, and their body language—but she was surprised. With some clients, she managed to go even deeper. They were looser in their own homes, more open. A woman who'd only ever talked about her job stood up in a session, turned the webcam toward the opposite wall, and showed Wendy a series of new paintings she'd done. That client had never so much as mentioned paintings before.

Wendy continued to see Allison, who had moved in with a new boyfriend and shifted her entire business online within days of the lockdown. She was as resilient as she'd ever been, and Wendy couldn't help but be proud of her. But Wendy had several clients who weren't doing so well.

One woman broke into tears in a session: an hour earlier, her twelve-year-old daughter had thrown an iPad at her head.

Another client had grown tired of isolating at home, logged on to Tinder, and slept with four strangers in the course of three days.

An older client, who'd just had her first grandchild, was devastated that it would be weeks, or months, or even longer, before she would be able to meet or hold the baby.

On most days it seemed to Wendy that the whole country—probably the whole world—was being traumatized, over and over again, and she resolved to be extra-mindful of her self-care regimen. In the past she had woken up early on Saturdays, driven to Malibu, and done yoga out on the beach. She had gone to the movies and spent as much time as she could in nature. Several times a year she flew to New York, where most of her family still lived. Now she took daily walks, talked to friends on the phone, and meditated. Wendy also increased the frequency of her supervision group's meetings, going from twice a month to once a week. Previously, she and her colleagues had consulted on cases. Now they spent more time discussing ways COVID had impacted their own lives, processing their own trauma, so that they could be more clear-minded with clients.

Wendy stuck to this new regimen for eleven weeks. And then, twelve weeks into the lockdown, she was confronted with one of the biggest challenges a therapist can face.

AT ONE POINT OR another in their careers, most social workers encounter a suicidal client. The experience can be frightening and overwhelming. Ideally it takes place in a psychiatric setting where the social worker belongs to a team and has good supervision. But suicidality is unpredictable. Social workers encounter it in family meetings, on home visits, over the phone, or in classrooms, and in these cases social workers find themselves on their own. It is their responsibility to determine the degree of danger their clients are in.

When speaking with a client who expresses suicidal thoughts of any kind, it is important to remain calm, listen actively, provide empathy, be direct and—perhaps most challenging for the social worker—not to overreact or un-derreact. "Suicidality" is an umbrella term encompassing suicidal thoughts, planning for suicide, and past suicide attempts, and while any expression of suicidality is extremely serious, there is a range of severity. Even in the best of times, there was no way to be certain of whether a client would act on his or her thoughts, and COVID-19 had made it more difficult to assess. Stress, anxiety, social isolation, depression, insomnia, and substance abuse had all become much more prevalent. In previous pandemics, going all the way back to the Black Death, suicide rates had gone up. It stood to reason that COVID-19 would cause them to rise, too. But at the outset of the pandemic, all of the evidence was anecdotal. No one knew for sure, and Wendy was taken aback when Ben, an old client, showed up on her computer screen looking haggard and drained.

Wendy had always known Ben to be lively and sharp, full of insight and empathy. He had a strong personality and plenty of charm. When she had first started seeing him, Ben had only just entered college—UCLA. Initially they had focused on his mother. Born in Ohio to an African American woman, Ben had been adopted at birth by a single Caucasian woman. He'd spent his childhood with her in Los Angeles, and the pair had an intensely close, occasionally volatile relationship. Despite their bond, Ben often wondered about his birth mother. He spoke about identity and how disorienting it had always been to be the only person of color at family gatherings. Sometimes he expressed anger at his mother for adopting him. "I had no say in being adopted," he'd point out. Then he'd felt guilt about being so angry. "She's dedicated her whole life to me," he would say. He desperately wanted to meet his birth mother but was deathly afraid of what he'd discover if they ever met.

Ben was dyslexic, too, and he had ADHD. He worried about failing or falling behind, and Wendy soon focused on his anxiety in those areas. All in all, they worked together for thirty-six months—well into Ben's junior year—and when he terminated his therapy, he was feeling good about school and felt more at peace with his adoption.

"I've been through a lot since the last time saw you," Ben told Wendy now.

It wasn't easy to tell over the webcam, but Wendy thought Ben's eyes looked glassy. He didn't look intoxicated, but he did seem remote, as if he were looking down from a great height. Wendy wished they could be in the same room, but they'd have to make do with the screen.

"Okay," she said, and let the pause linger.

"I never finished school," Ben said. "I dropped out senior year. But I got a job that I liked and they promoted me. Then I met Claire—which was good—but then she broke up with me . . ."

"Hold on," said Wendy. "You dropped out of college?"

"Senior year," Ben said. "Anyway, my mother died."

"Oh, Ben, I'm so sorry,"

Wendy felt Ben's loss in her gut, and her voice might have softened, but she tried to keep her expression neutral.

"When?" she asked.

"A month ago?"

Ben had been his mother's only child. She'd been his champion and anchor. "I worry about my mother worrying about me," he had told Wendy in one of their earliest sessions.

Ben's mother had died of COVID-19 on May 9, the day before Mother's Day. Ben hadn't been allowed into her hospital room to say goodbye. Afterward he had gone back to his childhood home, where he still had a bedroom.

Ben's aunts and uncles had handled the arrangements remotely.

"They couldn't have held a real funeral anyway," Ben said.

Ben had been furloughed from his job at the start of the pandemic. These days, he told Wendy, he barely got out of bed. His aunt Sarah stopped by several times a week; she insisted on bringing him food and watching him eat it. Sarah had always been Ben's favorite aunt. She had encouraged Ben to reach out to Wendy. In fact, she was somewhere in the house with him now.

"She freaked out when I told her I'd stopped taking Zoloft," Ben said.

For Wendy, this was like a bomb going off.

"When did you do that, Ben?"

"A couple of weeks ago. It wasn't working anyway."

Clinical social workers are not doctors—they cannot prescribe medication—but they are qualified to determine whether or not a client needs a referral for a psychiatrist. A person suffering from depression so severe that he can't get out of bed or shower, and who has difficulty working or sleeping, may well need to see a psychiatrist for medication to manage his symptoms. Best practice in these cases is a combination of medication and therapy, and part of Wendy's job involved knowing precisely whether or not a client would benefit from medication. If the answer was yes, she would secure a referral. But Ben's case was slightly different, because he'd gone *off* his medication on his own, and with Zoloft that could be dangerous. Zoloft was the kind of drug you had to taper off.

"Sarah's worried," Ben said. "But I told her I don't see the point."

"The point in what?" asked Wendy.

"In anything. I feel like we're all just waiting to die."

"Do *you* feel that way, Ben?"

"Sometimes. Especially lately."

For a new social worker, sitting with a suicidal client can be terrifying. Some of that terror does not go away, but Wendy had learned early on to keep asking questions, to be direct, and not to minimize or shy away from what the client was saying. As a young therapist her fear and insecurity might have impaired her ability to see Ben clearly. Wendy might even have joined him in his despair. But now she was equipped to help him. She asked a series of very blunt questions.

"Have you been sleeping?"

"Not really."

"Are you eating?"

"No."

"When was the last time you showered?"

"I can't remember."

Wendy paused for a moment and jotted down a few notes.

For the longest time, Wendy held the belief that people who committed suicide were depressed—that if their depression had been treated, the impulse to end their lives would have been dispelled. The truth is a client who is severely depressed may be *less* likely to harm herself: there's such a thing as feeling so hopeless that you can't go through with the thing. Someone who might be impulsive and mildly depressed or even manic actually presents a much higher risk. Ben seemed to fall into the first category, but Wendy needed to be sure.

"Ben," she said gently, "have you had any thoughts that scare you?"

For the first time since saying "Hello," Ben lifted his eyes up and looked directly into the webcam.

"I don't want to tell you. You'll send me to a hospital. You can't send me to a hospital now."

Most social workers in private practice have a voice mail

that ends: "If this is an emergency, please hang up and dial 911." This is because, at the end of the day, a social worker's ability to hospitalize a suicidal client or avert a suicide attempt is limited. In certain cases, when a social worker determines that a client poses an imminent danger to him- or herself or others—when he or she is threatening to jump out of a window or has a gun—the social worker herself will call 911. But in real life such immediate code-red situations are extremely rare.

Whatever Ben may have thought, Wendy would not have automatically sent a client with suicidal ideation to the hospital.

In fact, social workers are not required by law to hospitalize such patients; nor do they have the power to have clients committed. What social workers do have is an ethical responsibility to evaluate whether or not the person in front of them is a danger to him- or herself and identify the level and immediacy of the danger. They have a responsibility to create a concrete safety plan, to consult with colleagues on the client and the plan, and to recommend hospitalization if needed. It is also crucially important, for purposes of malpractice, that a social worker in any setting document each of these efforts.

was concerned, if Ben wanted to harm himself, a piece of paper saying he would not do so wasn't going to stop him.

Instead, Wendy decided to have a real conversation about resources—both internal and external—that Ben could summon immediately to help him feel more hopeful and less alone.

Wendy took note of Ben's honesty. He had reached out to her for a reason. He wasn't giving her many details, but he'd been quite open about his mood, his thoughts, and his feelings. Dark as those feelings were, his candor was encouraging. Flat as his affect was, there was a part of Ben that *wanted* help.

"Ben," Wendy said, "did you say Sarah's in the house with you?"

"She's in the living room. She didn't want to leave me."

"Would you feel comfortable having her join our conversation so we can come up with a plan to be sure that you're safe?"

It took just a bit of nudging to get Ben to agree.

Together with Sarah, they came up with a plan. Sarah would stay at the house. She'd make sure that Ben went to a psychiatrist to discuss trying some new medications. When the world opened up again, she'd take Ben to get a full physical—something Wendy always recommended—to

If a social worker does recommend hospitalization
the client agrees, the social worker is more likely to c
a family member for support than to escort a client t
hospital personally. For liability reasons—What if the
dives into oncoming traffic while the social worker's
to hail a cab to take the client to the hospital?—some
cies even have policies prohibiting their social worke
accompanying clients to an emergency room.

Moreover, hospitalization is no guarantee that
clients won't follow through with their intentions i
ately upon discharge. A hospital may not assess a cli
oughly enough or keep them long enough for medi
take effect. If a client's determination to kill him-
doesn't waver with intervention and a hospital sta
worker can't stop it. Taking all of this into accoun
felt the best tool she had at her disposal while talk
wasn't hospitalization: it was her ability to connec
to acknowledge his despair, to gain his trust, a
collaboratively with him to develop a plan to kee

Wendy could have drawn up a safety contract
all of the agencies and hospitals she had worked i
col for assessing suicidal clients always included
and documentation of such a contract. But as

rule out other causes of depression. In the meantime Sarah would make sure that Ben followed up with Wendy.

When the call ended, Wendy shut her laptop, closed her eyes, ran through a series of quick breathing exercises, and pictured herself doing yoga on the beach. Given the circumstances, she felt she had set Ben on the best possible course. It had been a tough call, deciding against hospitalization. But, she thought, it was correct.

An hour later her cell phone rang. Wendy was still making notes in Ben's chart, but he had already called the psychiatrist she'd recommended. The man was expensive, Ben said. Out of network. He had also insisted that Ben see him for medication management and weekly psychotherapy. That was too much for Ben. He didn't have the financial resources. Wendy agreed. She told Ben she would call him back.

After an hour making calls on his behalf, she'd gotten Ben a virtual appointment at an in-network clinic for the very next day. Upon calling him back, she suggested that they register for the appointment together. They spent the next half hour filling forms out online. Before she hung up, Wendy asked Ben to confirm that Sarah would be there for the actual appointment. She went to bed late that night, tired but also relieved, and slept soundly.

SOCIAL WORK IS NEVER easy. With the pandemic, it had become twice as exhausting, twice as hard. There would be other nights when Wendy would hardly sleep at all. There would be days when she herself would break down crying. On those days Wendy would let herself sit with the feeling until her head cleared. Then she would log back on to Zoom, where she needed to be, because even in extreme circumstances she had to be present for her clients. That was the job, after all—a job Wendy loved because it made her feel more connected, more alive than anything else she had done.

Some social workers live by the mantra, "You should never work harder than your client." Wendy doesn't agree. "Sometimes you do have to work harder than your client," she says. "Sometimes you have to help clients more than they help themselves—because there are times when the client just can't manage. It might be difficult work, and you might find yourself doing it at the end of a long day, and you might be very tired. But your clients will wake you up anyway. Something will happen in a session, like it did with Ben, and you think, 'I'm awake now. I'm awake.'"

FURTHER READING

Social workers are avid readers, always on the lookout for books that might change their thinking, expand their understanding of people in their environments, and resonate within their practice. Here are some books which did that for our social workers:

The Lost Children of Wilder:
The Epic Struggle to Change Foster Care
by Nina Bernstein

This history of a landmark class action lawsuit—one that transformed foster care—delves into the personal stories behind that case as it highlights the ways that our foster care system brutalizes children it's meant to protect.

All God's Children:
The Bosket Family and the American Tradition of Violence
by Fox Butterfield

While tracing one family's roots back to their days as enslaved people in South Carolina, Butterfield makes a convincing case for the European—specifically, the Scotch-Irish—origins of inner-city violence. *All God's Children* isn't as well-known as it should be, but it is fascinating and essential.

The Spirit Catches You and You Fall Down:
A Hmong Child, Her American Doctors,
and the Collision of Two Cultures
by Anne Fadiman

When their infant girl is diagnosed with severe epilepsy, the members of her immigrant family in California are forced to navigate Western medical systems they find utterly foreign and mystifying. Among other things, Fadiman's investigation is an elegant, heartbreaking primer on the importance of cultural humility.

Trauma and Recovery:
The Aftermath of Violence—
From Domestic Abuse to Political Terror
by Judith Lewis Herman

Based on historical case studies as well as the author's own experience as a clinical psychiatrist, this smart, incisive book draws a line between individual traumas (rape, child sexual abuse) and historical disasters (wars, terrorist attacks), providing clear, measured advice for therapists working with survivors of violence and clients suffering from PTSD.

Hood Feminism:
Notes from the Women That a Movement Forgot
by Mikki Kendall

This bracing look at the ways in which the women's movement has left women of color behind is essential to understanding the limits that violence, food insecurity, inadequate housing, and the lack of educational opportunities places on impoverished populations.

Drinking: A Love Story
by Caroline Knapp

Knapp's honest, unflinching memoir details her decades-long struggle with alcohol. It's full of valuable insights for anyone working in addiction recovery.

The Body Keeps the Score:
Brain, Mind, and Body in the Healing of Trauma
by Bessel van der Kolk

Traumatic experiences have lifelong effects on our bodies as well as our minds—but, in the course of rewiring our brains, we can let go of that physical fallout. Van der Kolk's book is a road map and a survival manual based on innovative treatments and cutting-edge scientific research.

There Are No Children Here:
The Story of Two Boys Growing Up in the Other America
by Alex Kotlowitz

Two brothers grow up in the Henry Horner Homes, on Chicago's west side, in this immersive look at the brutal, relentless effects of entrenched poverty, violence, and social decay.

Random Family:
Love, Drugs, Trouble, and Coming of Age in the Bronx
by Adrian Nicole LeBlanc

LeBlanc spent ten years immersed in the lives of Jessica, Coco, their lovers, their friends, and their family members in New York's poorest borough. Like Alex Kotlowitz, she emerged with a searingly intimate, devastating portrait of a marginalized community.

Trauma Stewardship:
An Everyday Guide to Caring for Self
While Caring for Others
by Laura van Dernoot Lipsky
with Connie Burk

How can people who work with trauma minimize the amount they absorb? Van Dernoot Lipsky and Burk examine the symptoms of secondary trauma and burnout while offering practical tools for building resilience and restoring balance.

The Man Who Mistook His Wife for a Hat
and Other Clinical Tales
by Oliver Sacks

These histories of patients struggling with bizarre neurological abnormalities read like finely crafted short stories. They're inspiring, too, because, in the end, Sacks's subjects prove to be as adaptive as they are impaired.

The Center Cannot Hold:
My Journey Through Madness
by Elyn R. Saks

Saks was eight when she experienced her first moments of psychosis. At twenty-eight, she was diagnosed with schizophrenia. In time, after multiple hospitalizations and years of treatment, she learned to manage her illness and thrived, becoming a well-respected law professor and MacArthur "Genius Grant" winner.

And the Band Played On:
Politics, People, and the AIDS Epidemic
by Randy Shilts

Shilts's classic history of the AIDS epidemic is also a sobering look at the ways in which Americans of all stripes failed to respond to the crisis. Sadly, it's no less relevant today than it was when first published in 1987.

The Noonday Demon:
An Atlas of Depression
by Andrew Solomon

This deeply personal, exhaustively researched look at the history, science, and politics of depression moves effortlessly between research, reportage, and accounts of Solomon's own lifelong struggle with mental illness.

Caste:
The Origins of Our Discontents
by Isabel Wilkerson

Wilkerson—author of a celebrated history of the Great Migration—turns the idea of race upside down and looks at caste as the unspoken but dominant factor in American history and American lives. "Caste is the bones," she writes, "race the skin."

ABOUT THE AUTHORS

Alex Abramovich is the author of *Bullies: A Friendship*. He writes for the *London Review of Books* and teaches at Columbia University.

Tasha Blaine is a social worker and the author of *Just Like Family: Inside the Lives of Nannies, the Parents They Work for, and the Children They Love*. She lives and works in New York City.